ADULT COLORING BOOK

Animal Edition

By Jeremy Laszlo

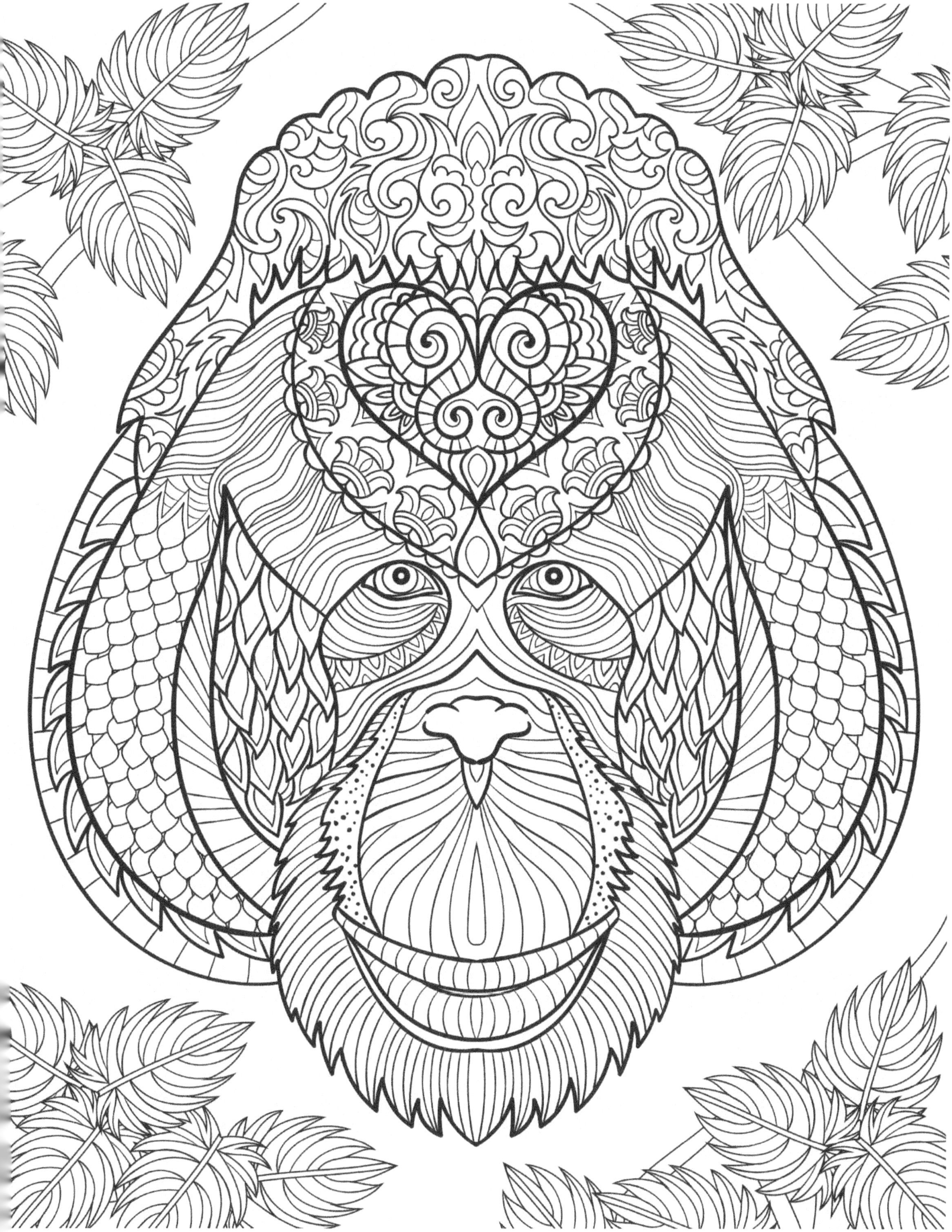

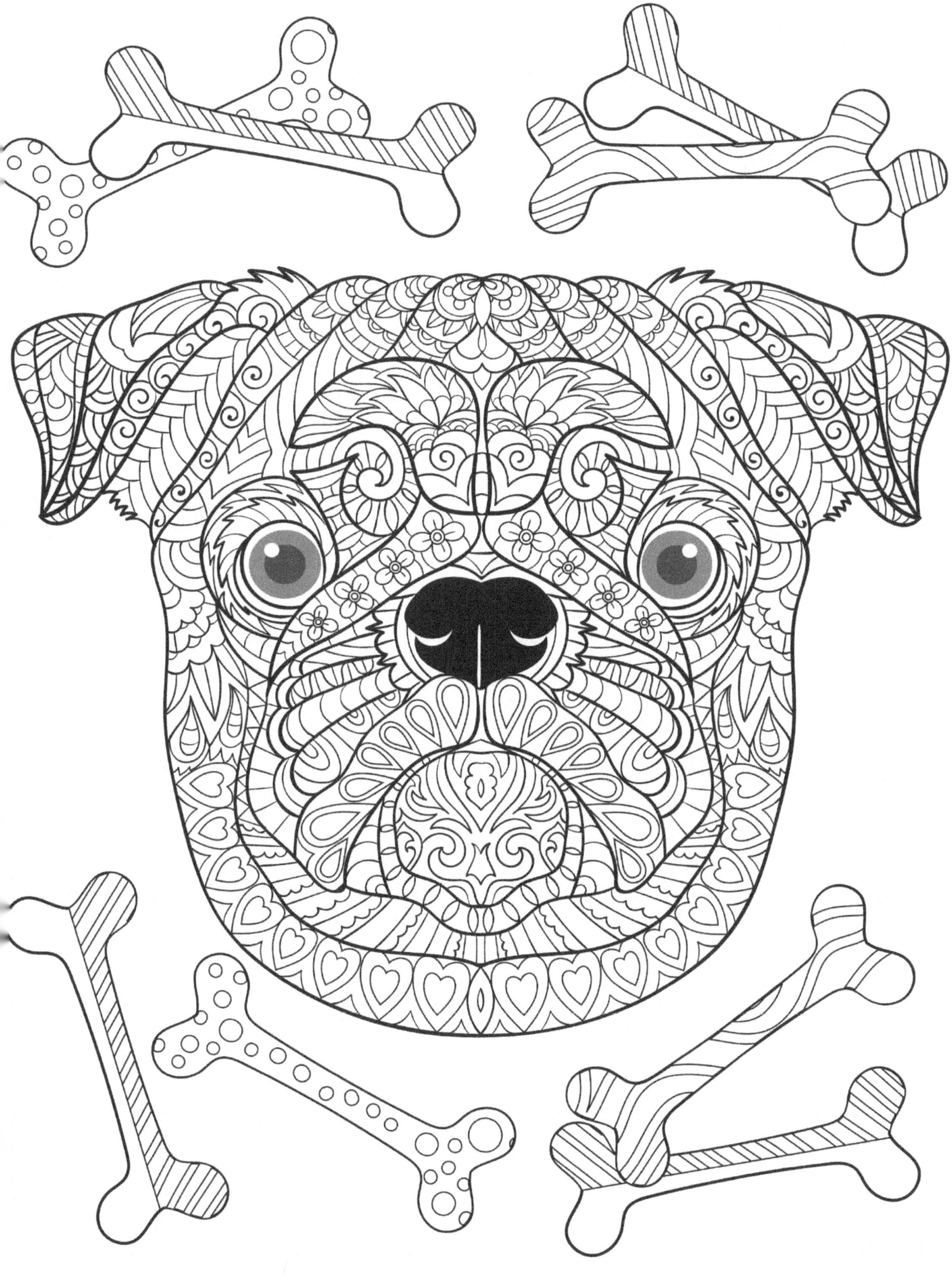

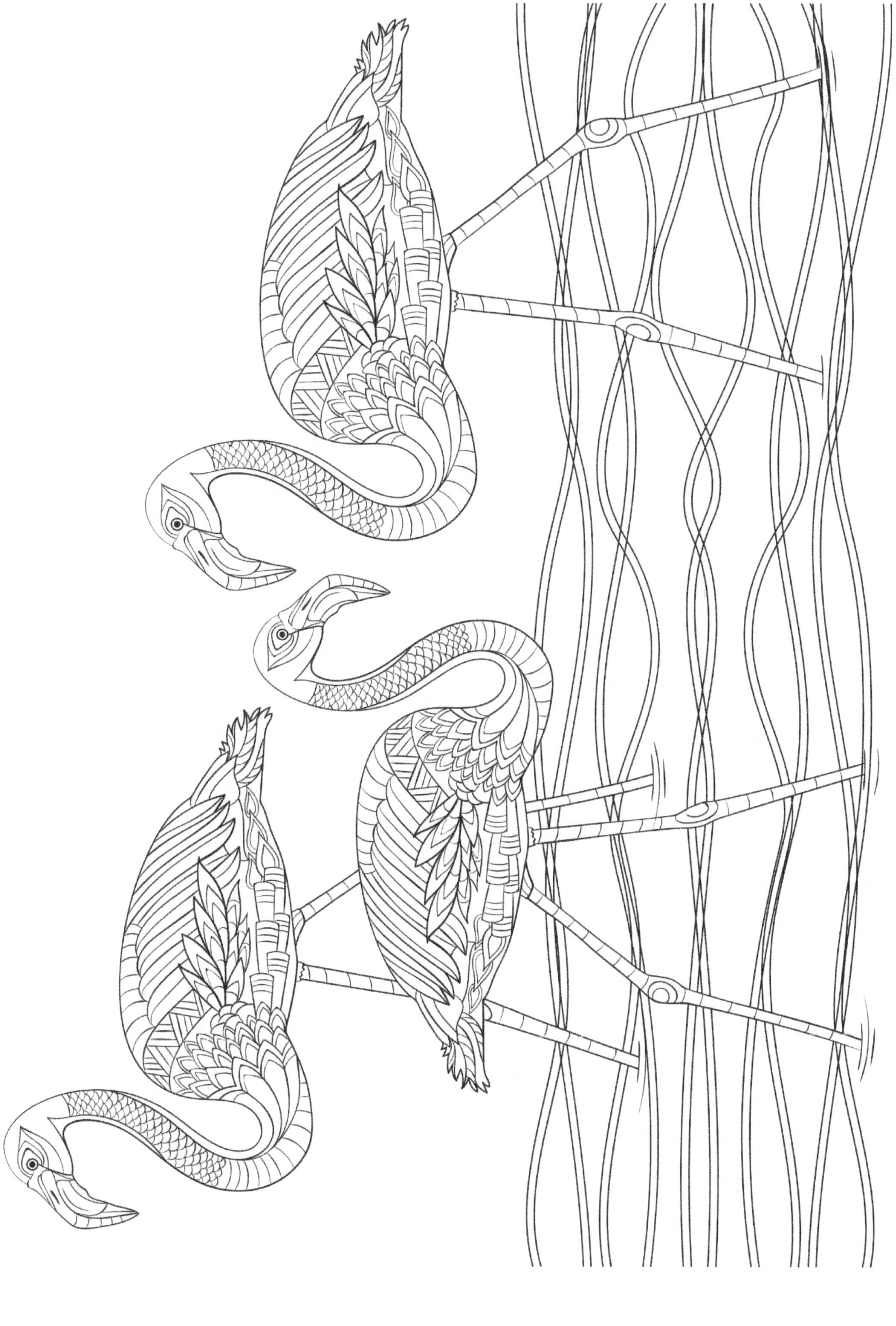

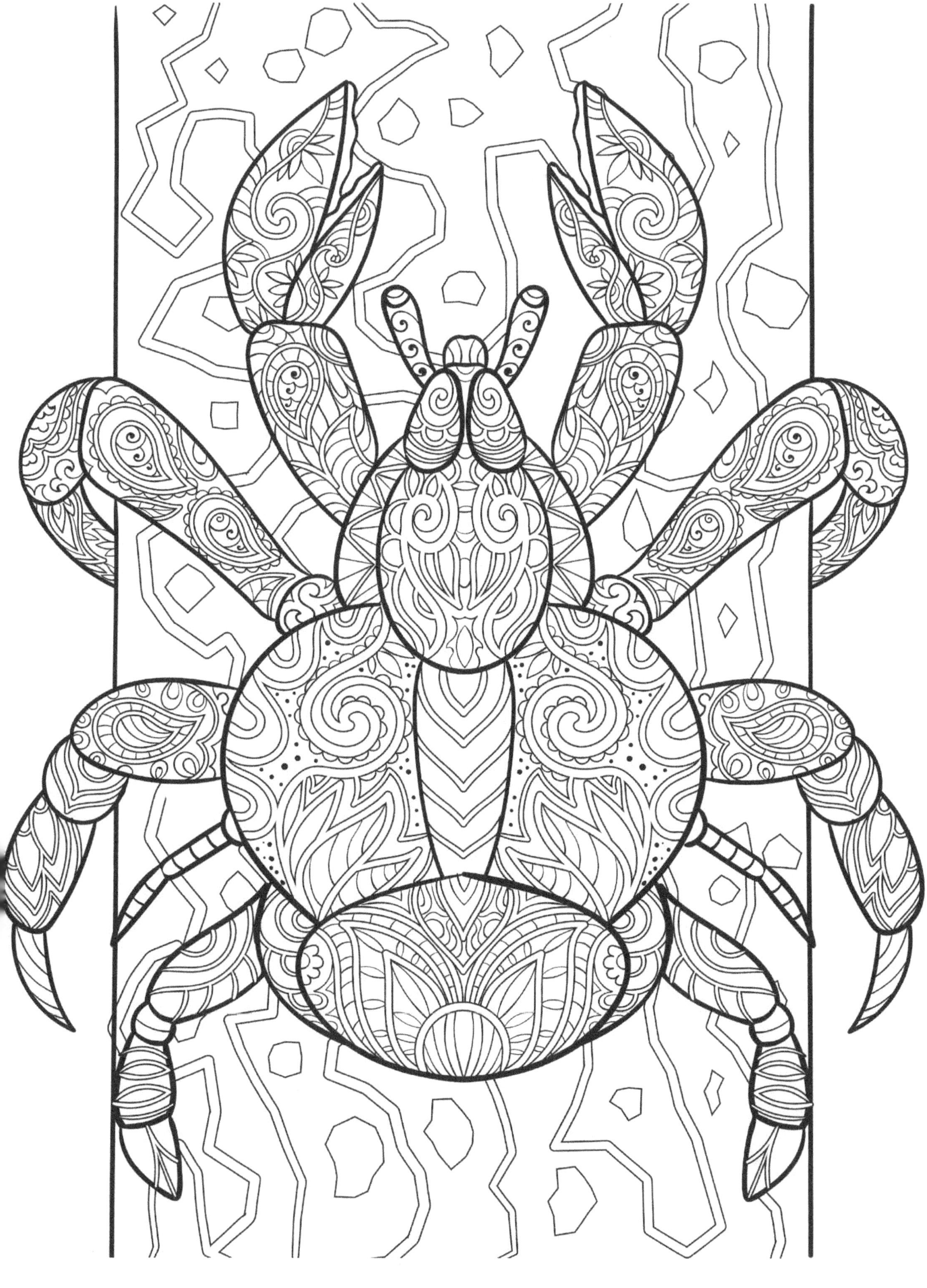

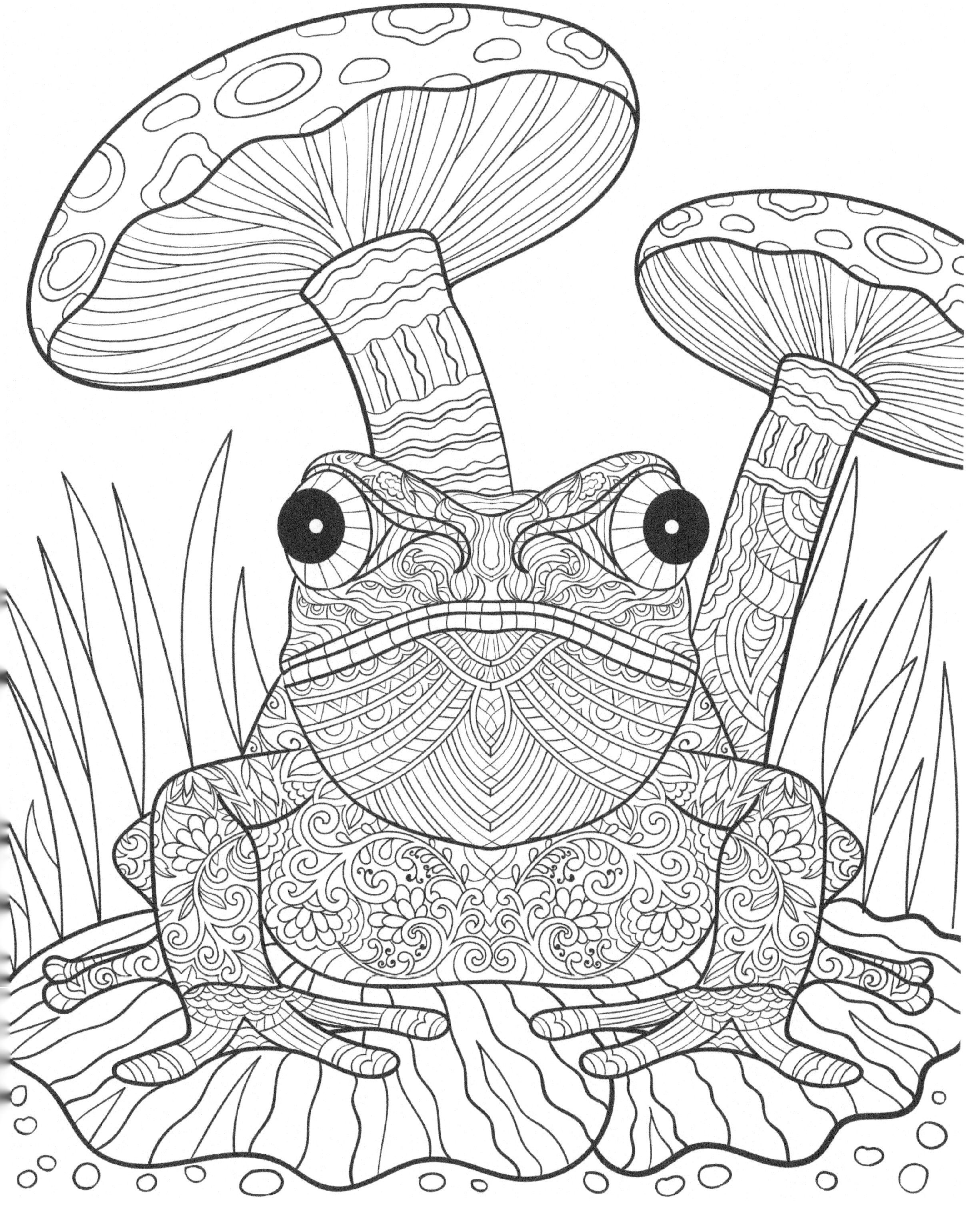

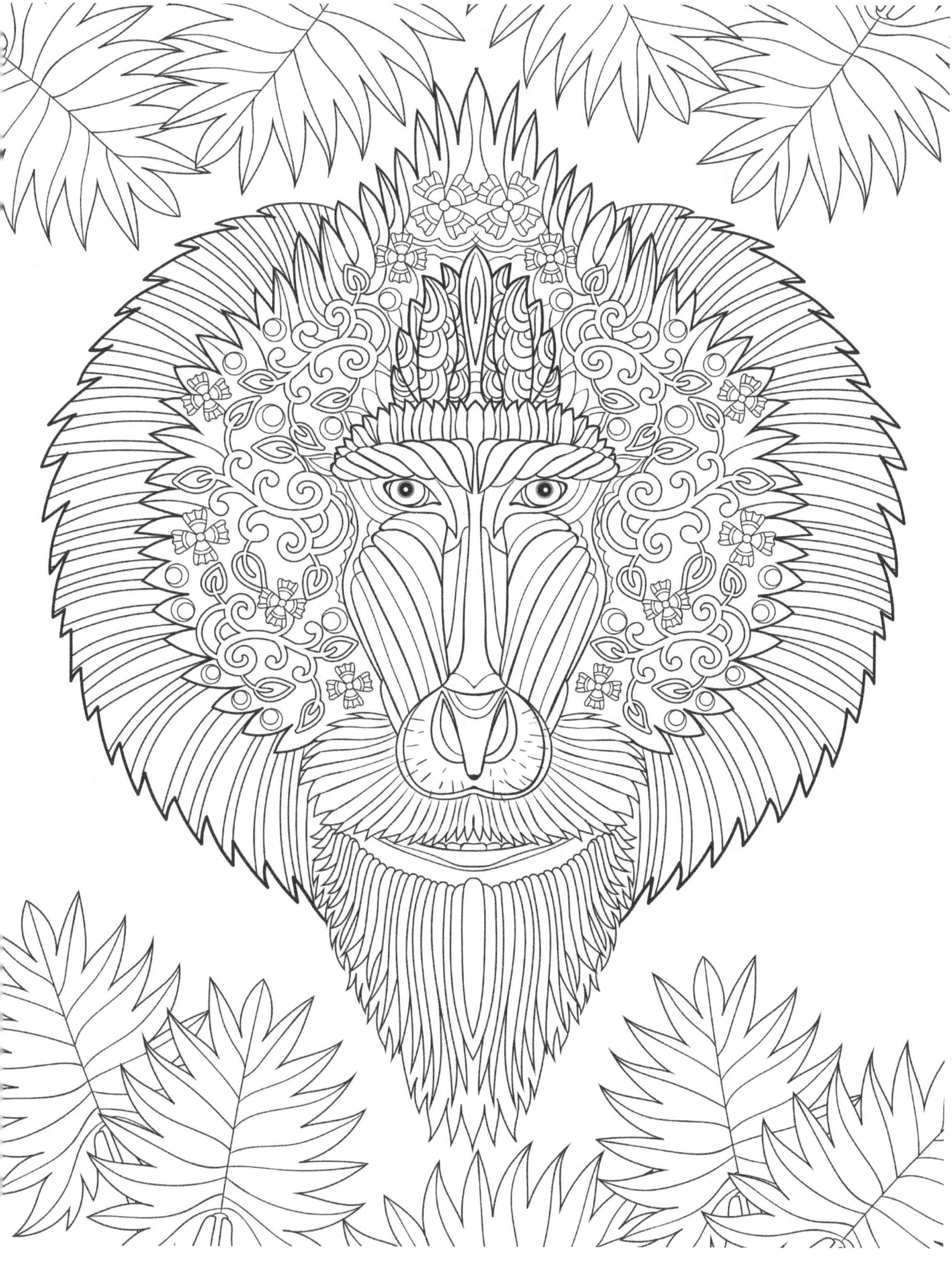

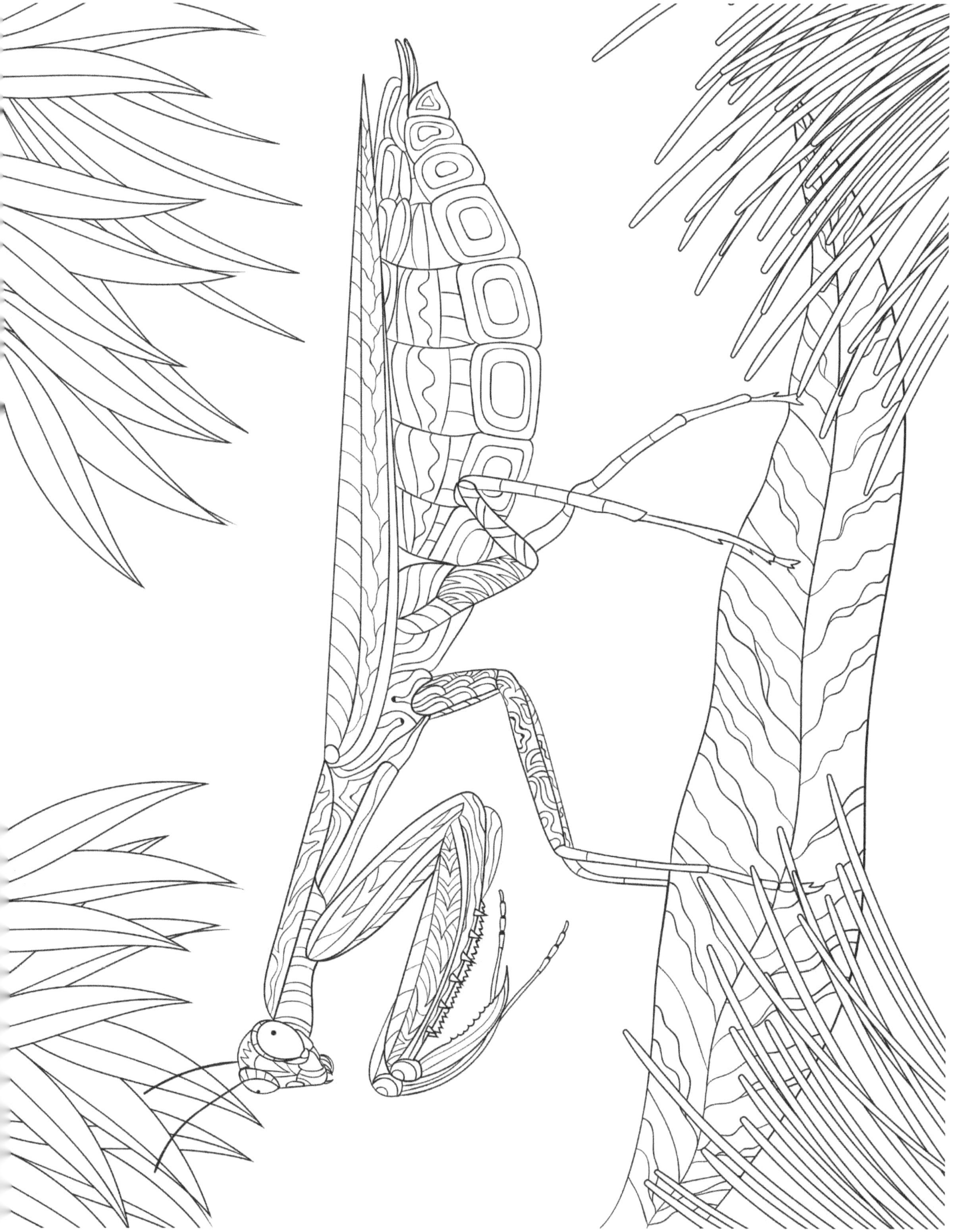

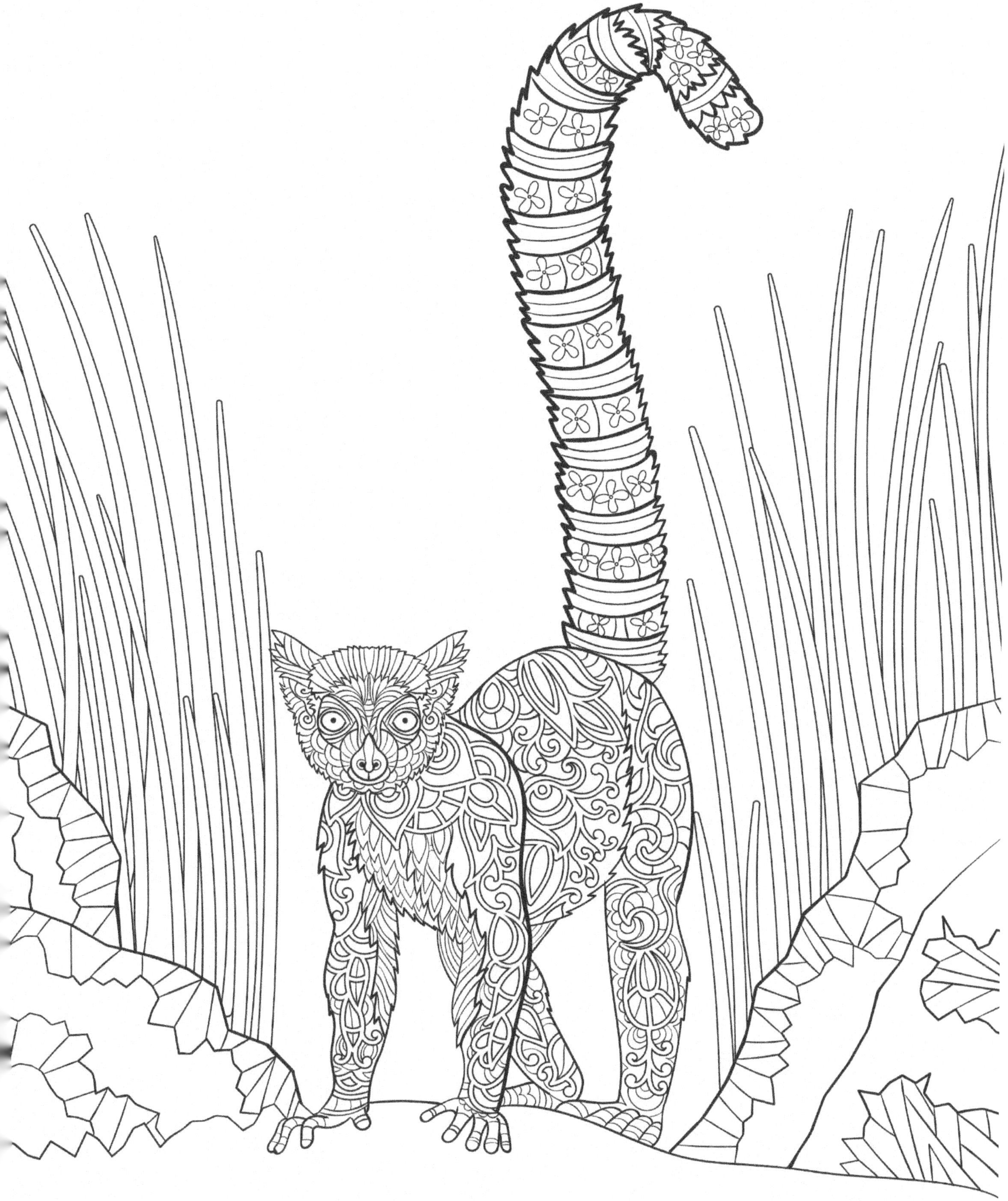

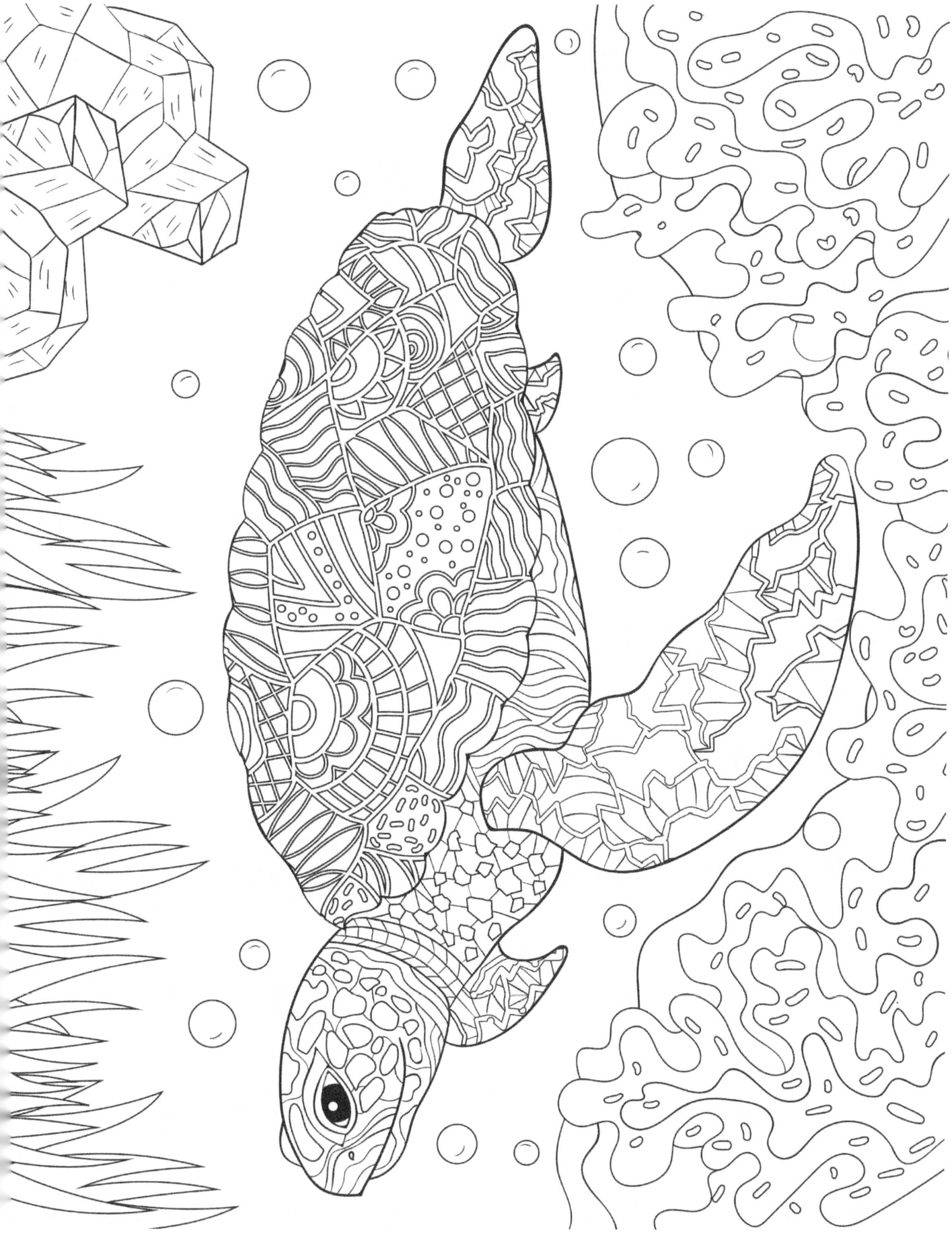

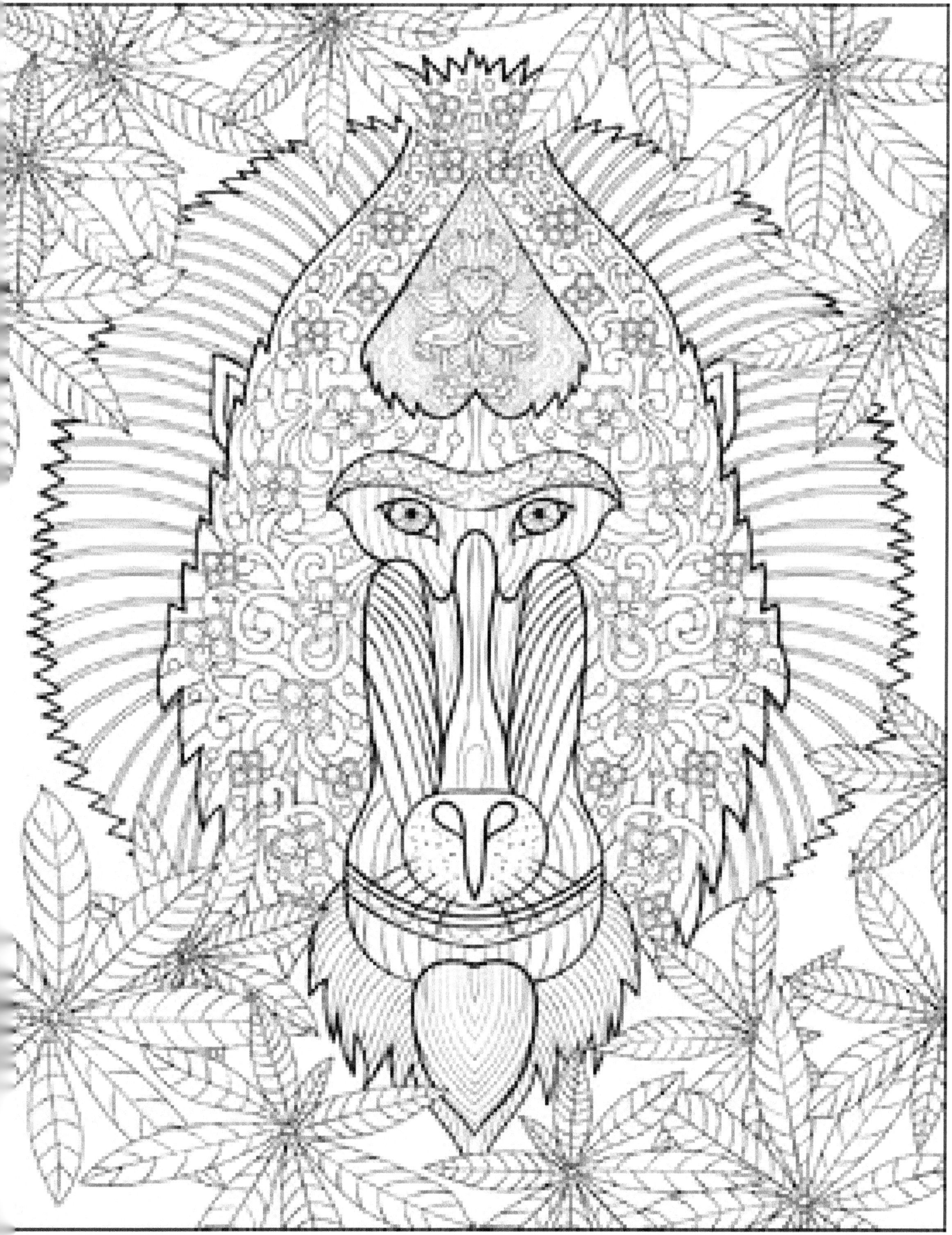

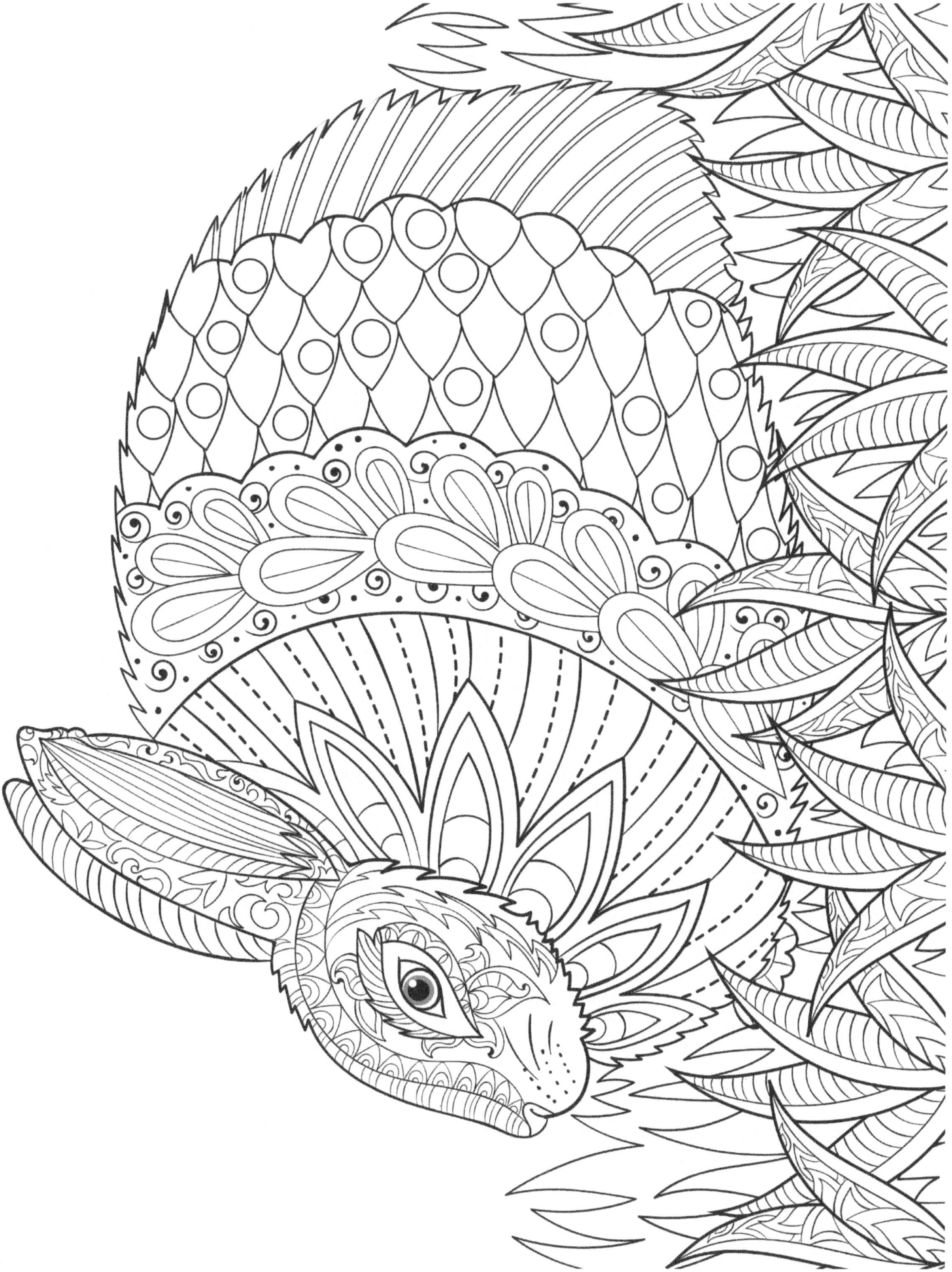

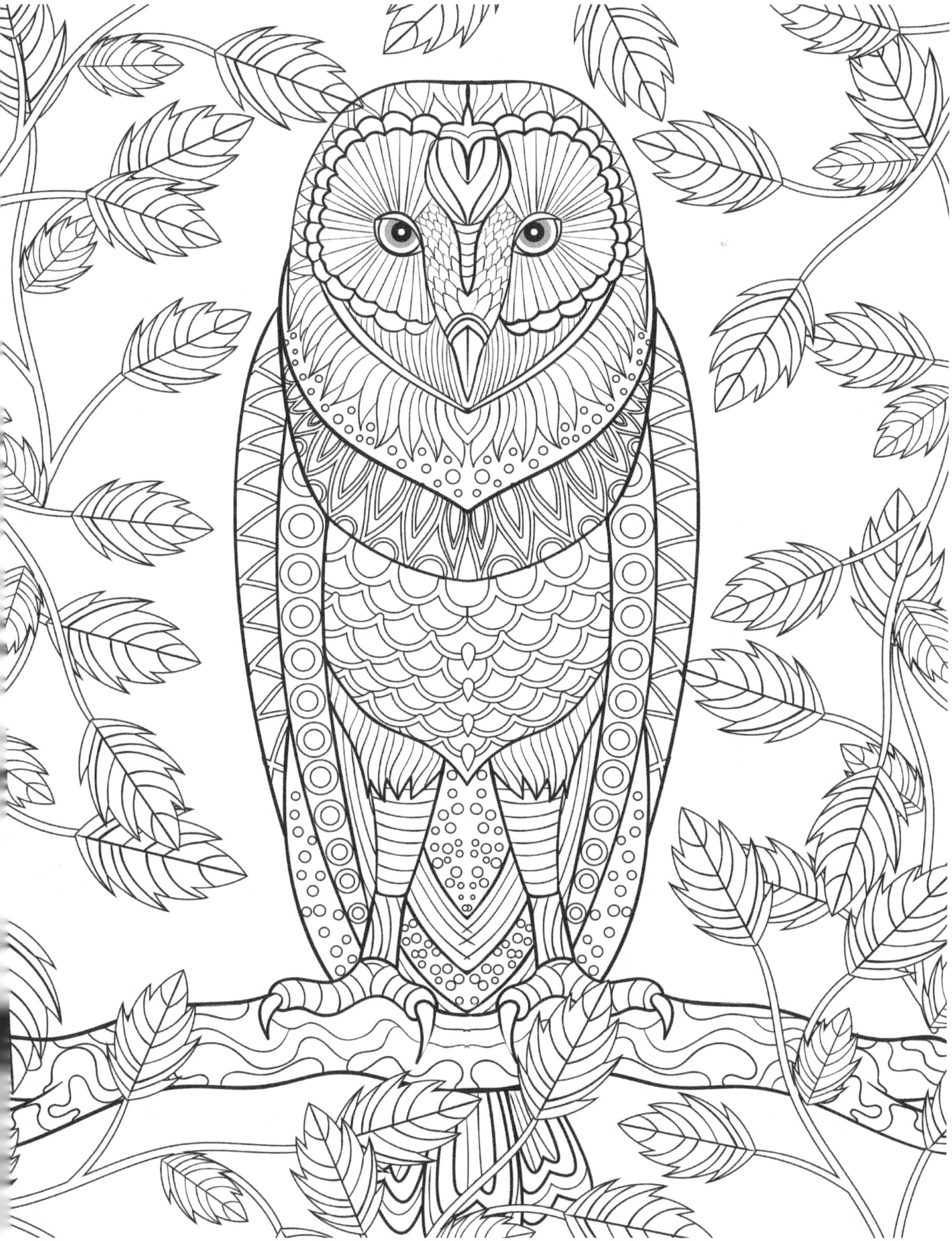

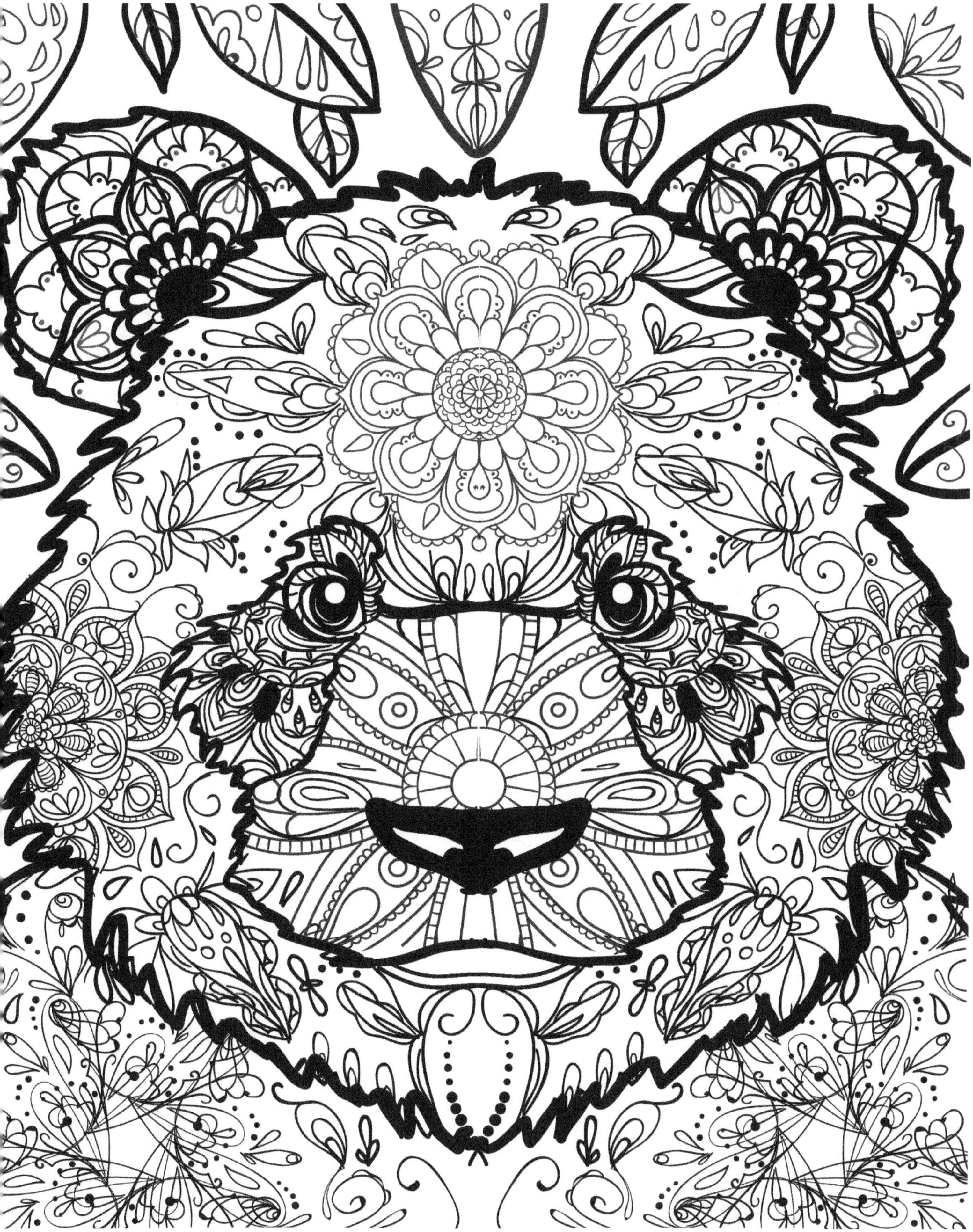

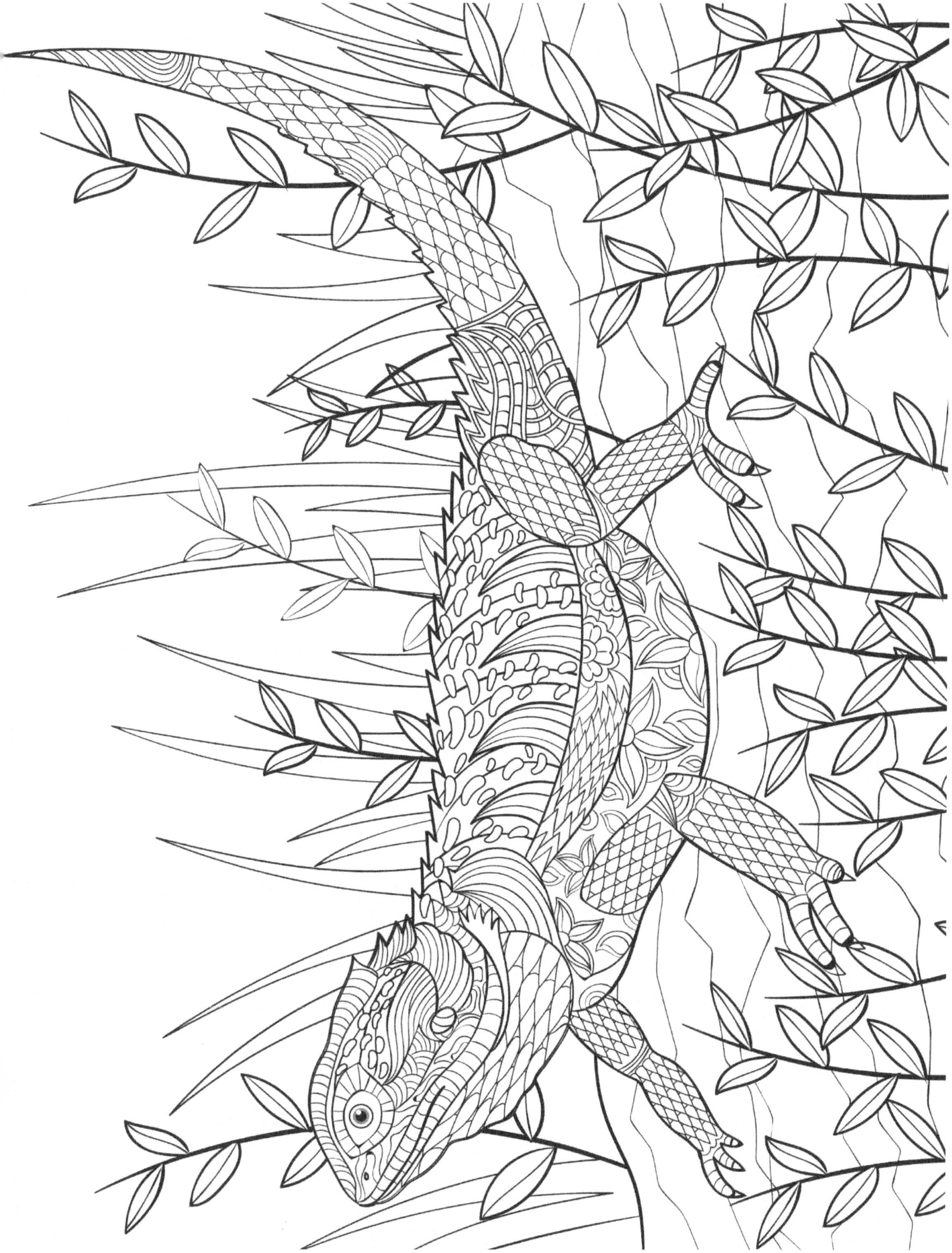

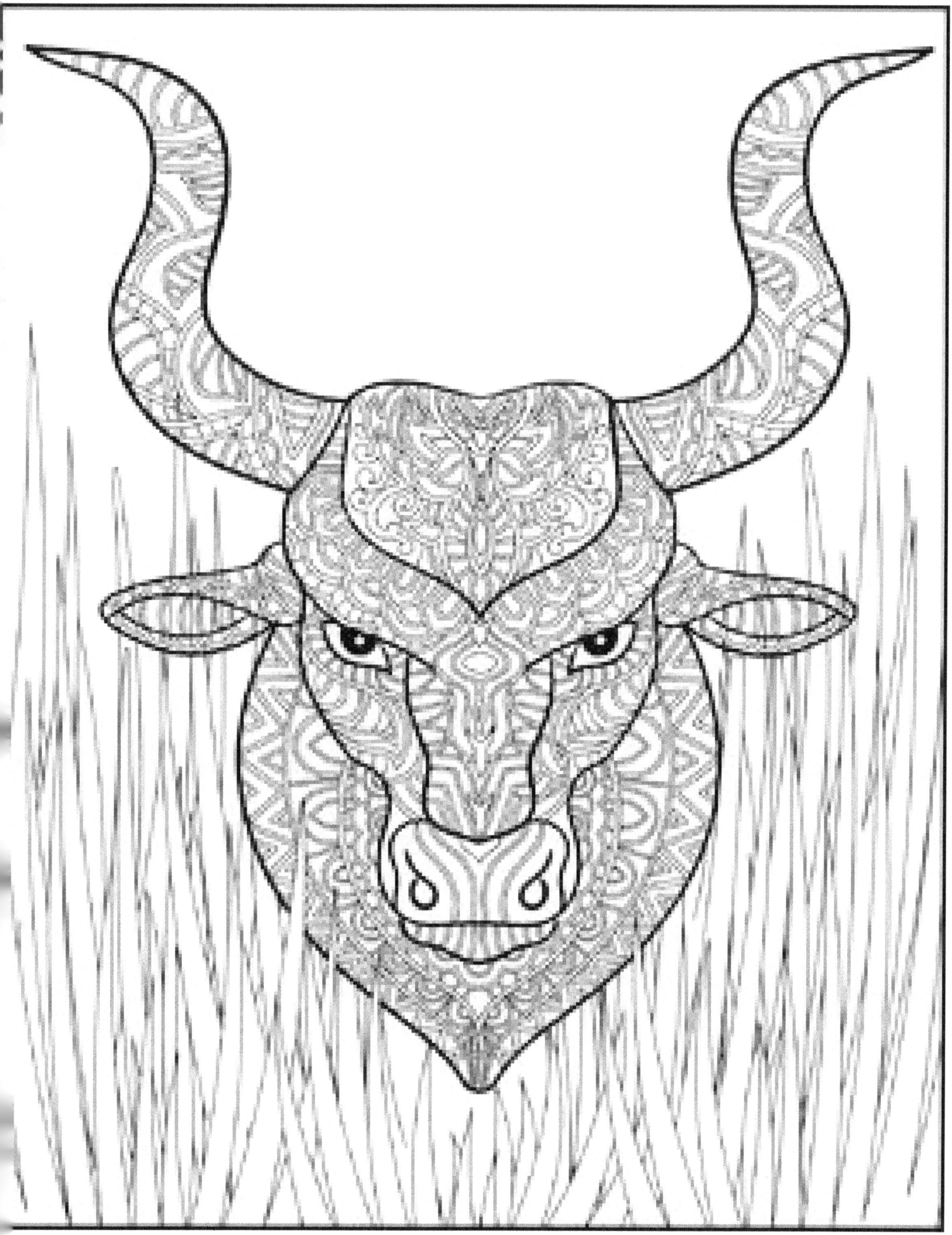

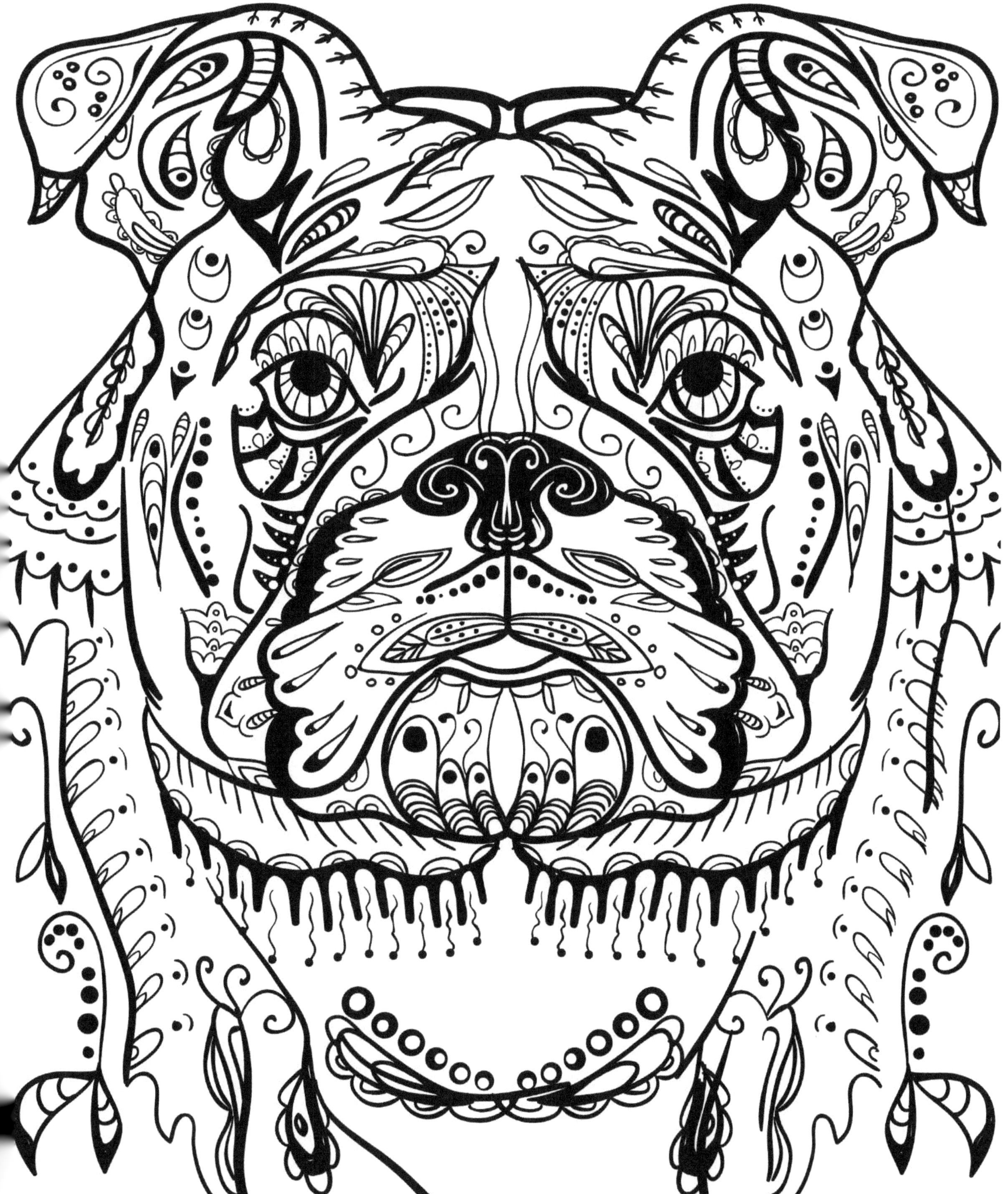

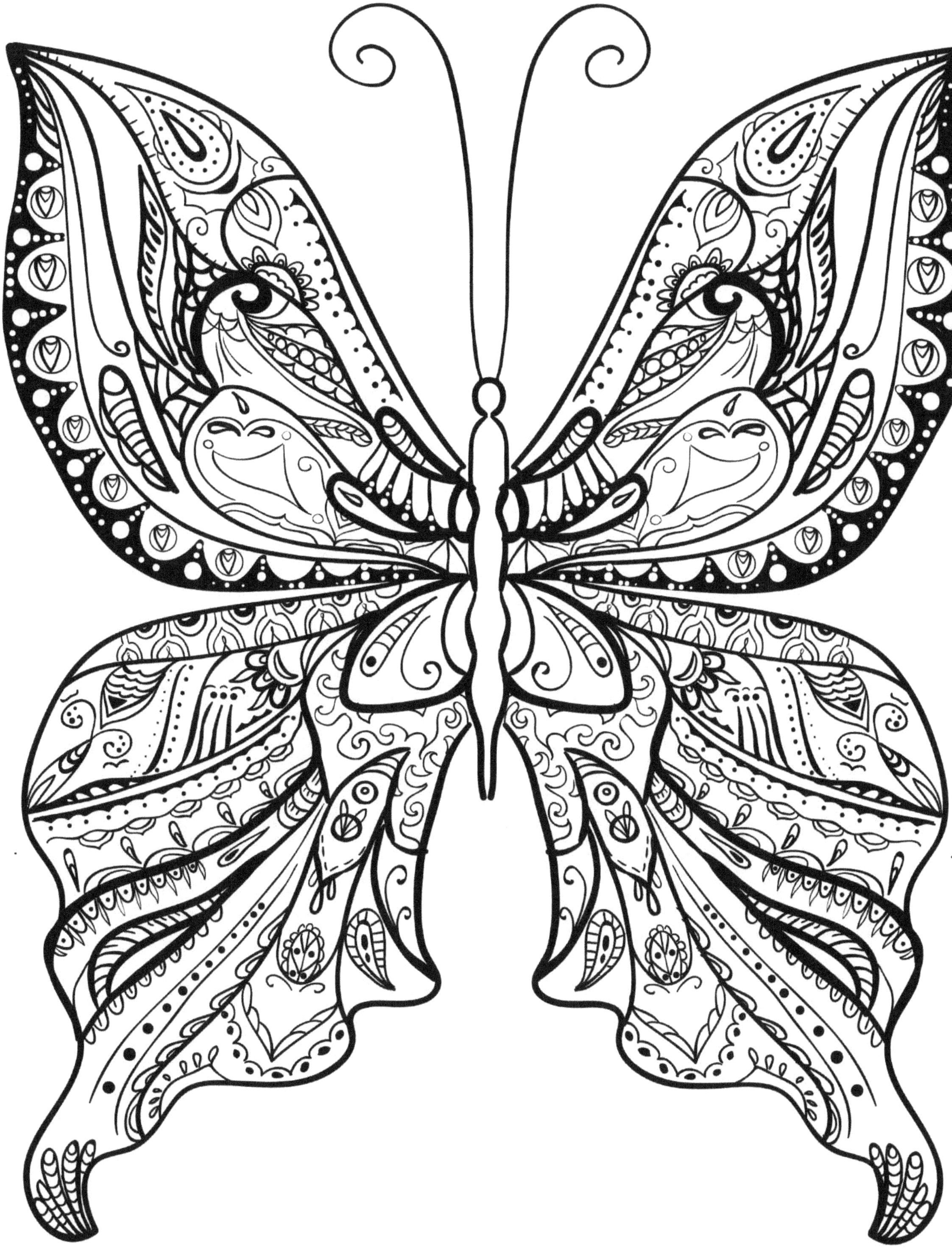

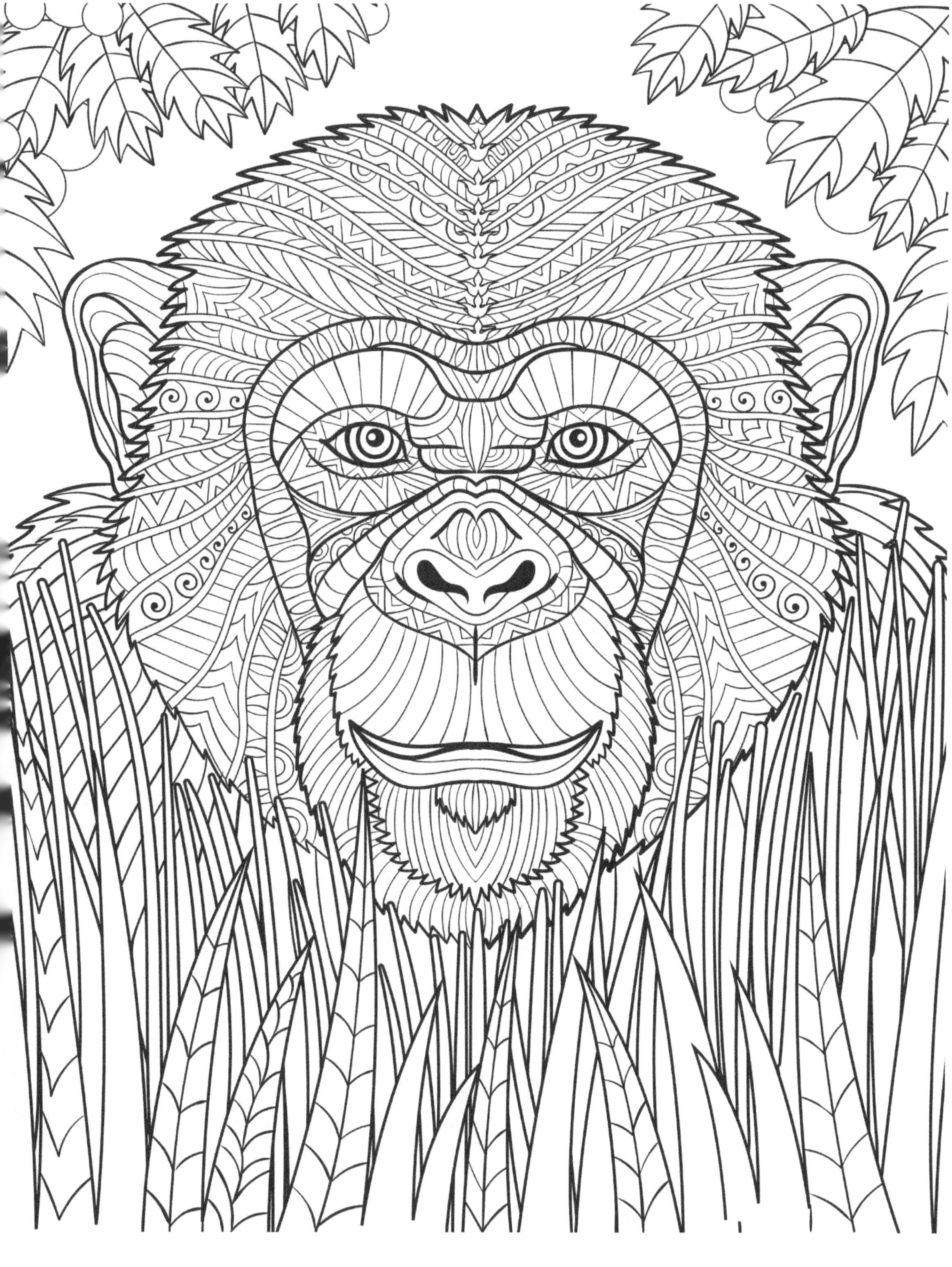

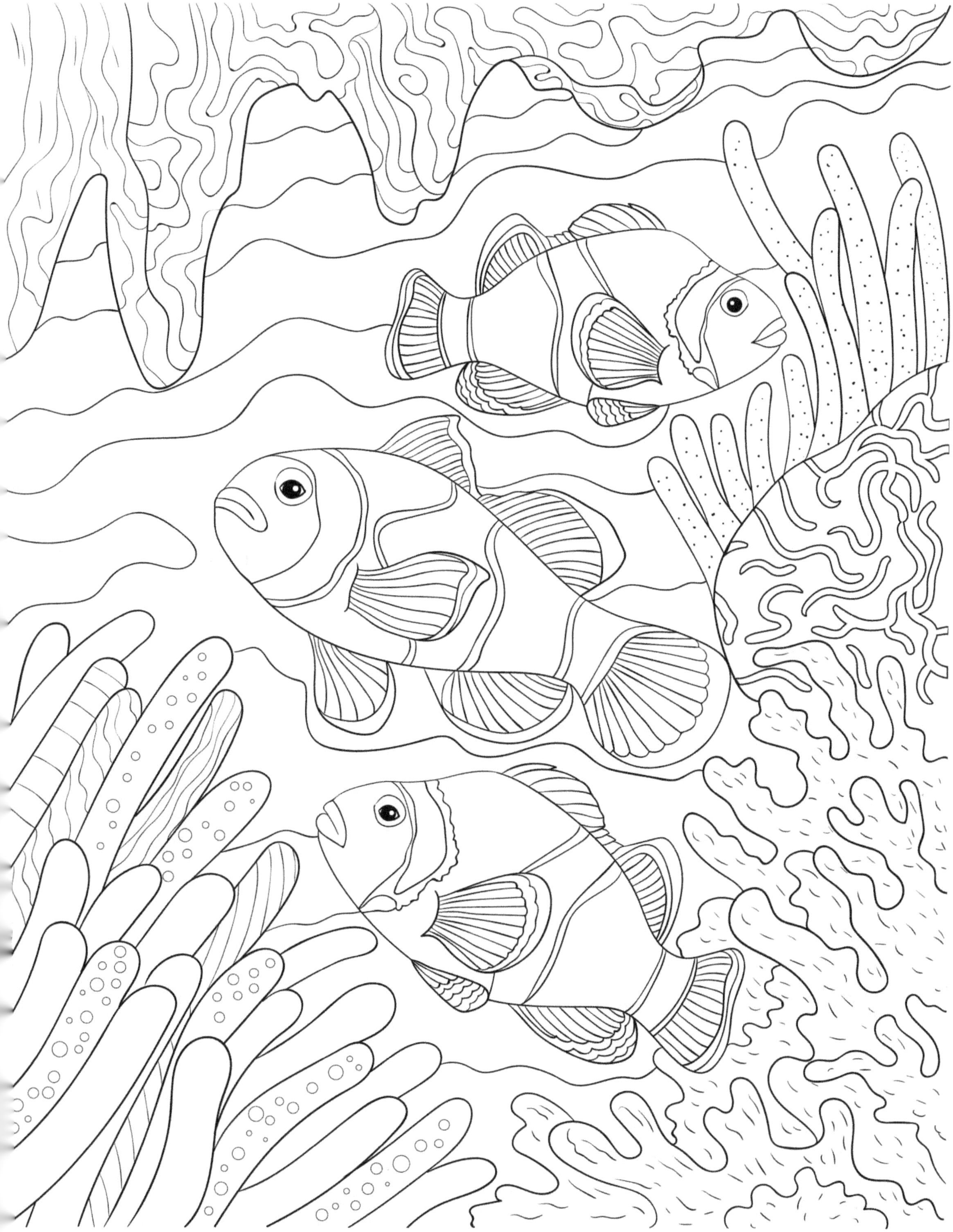

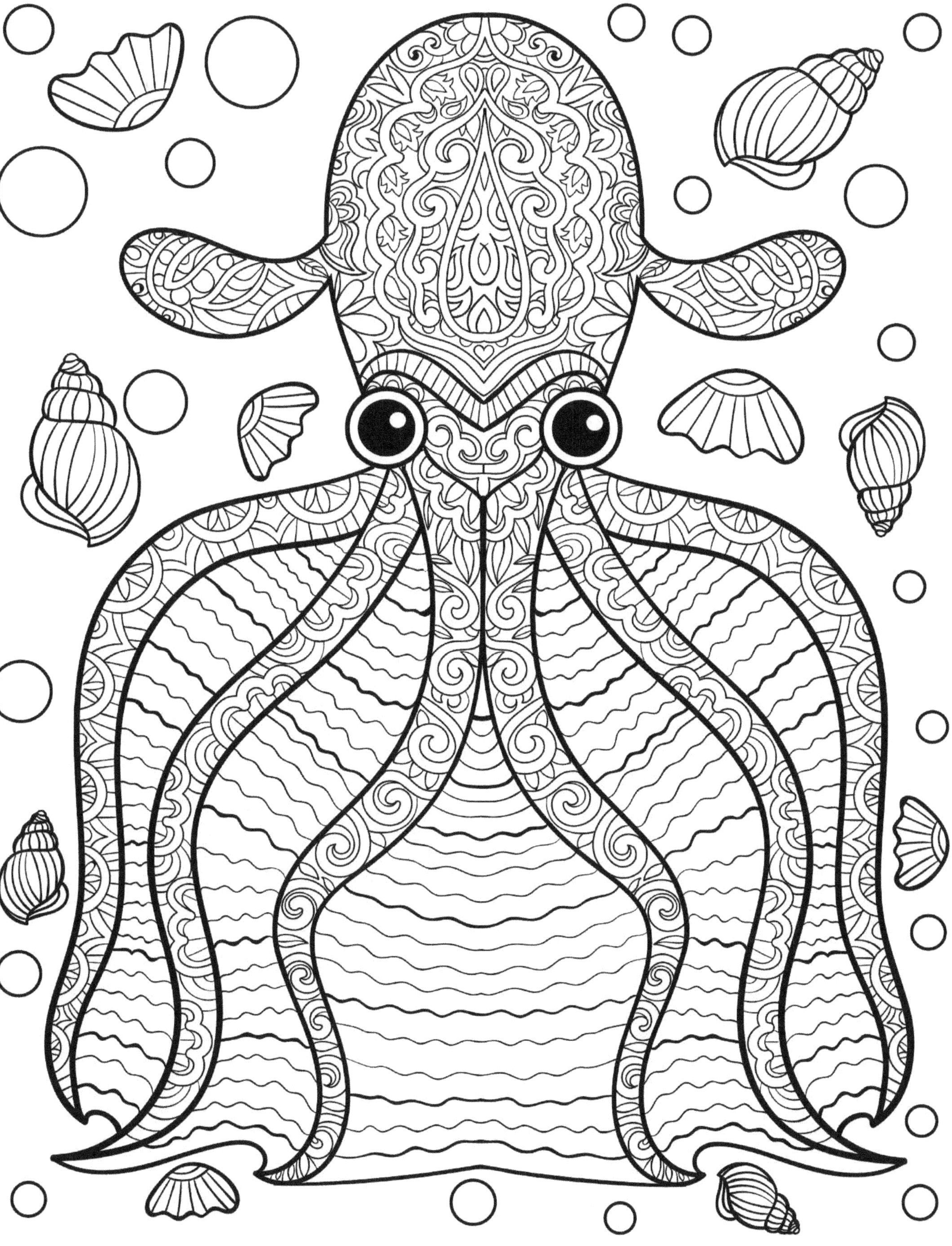

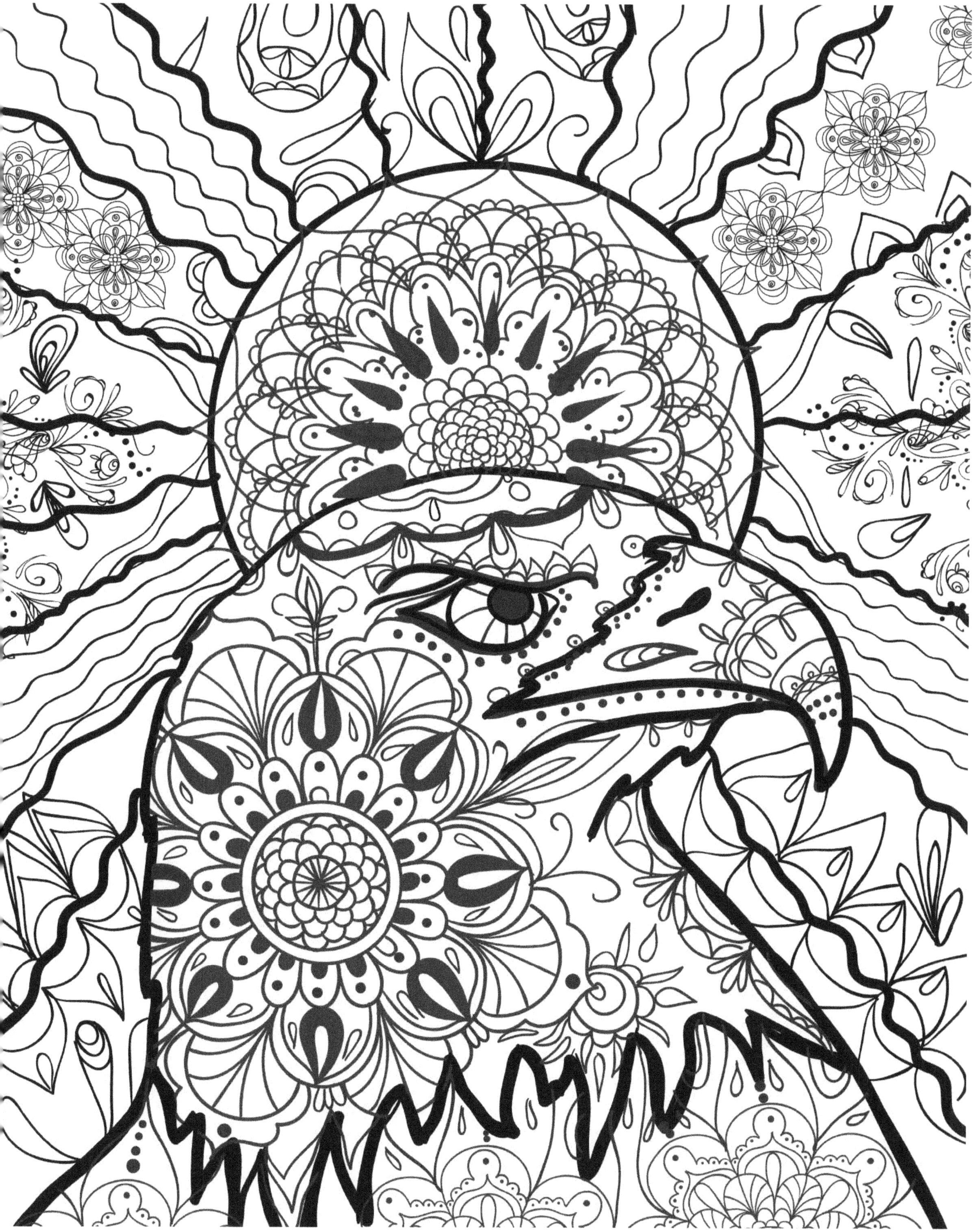

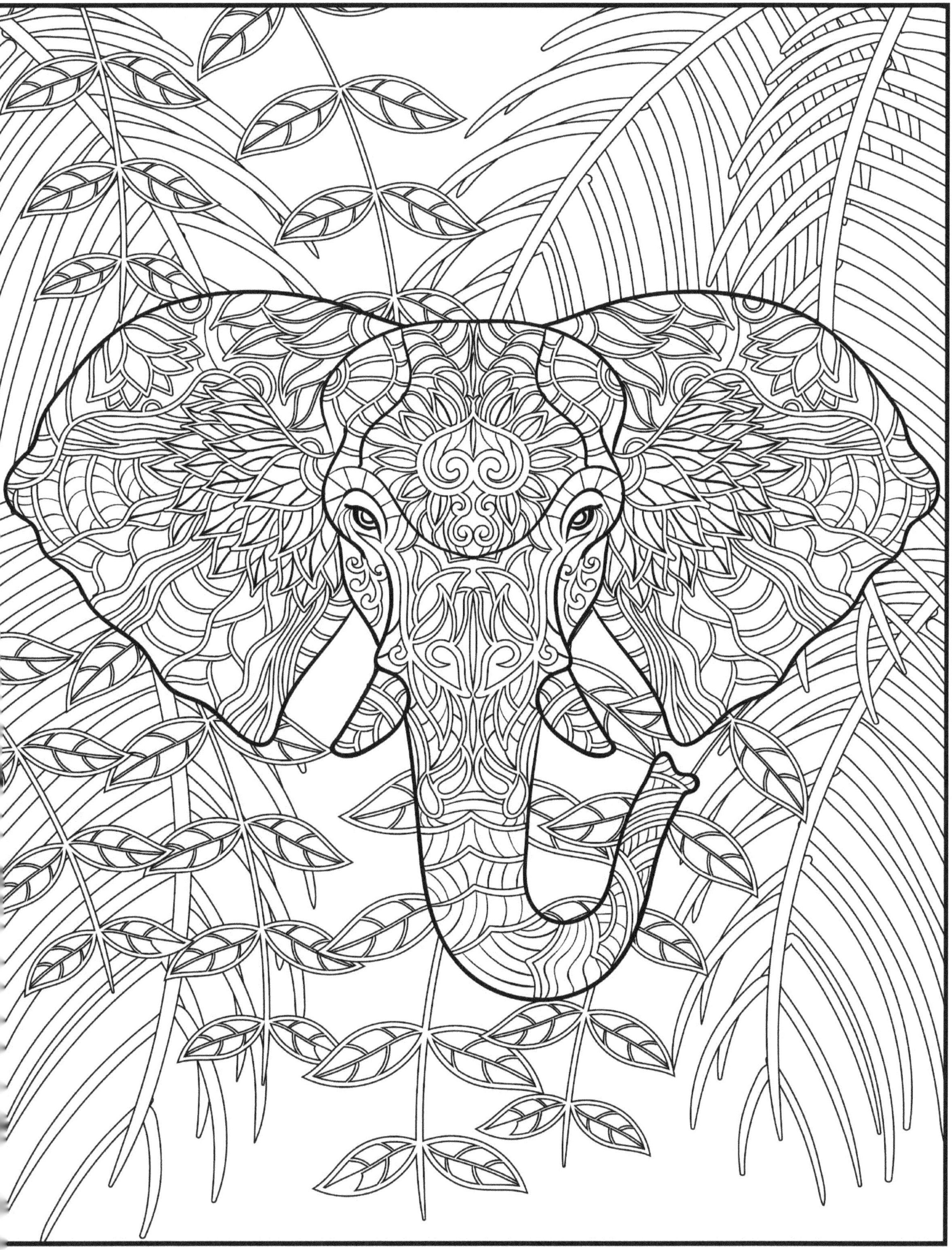

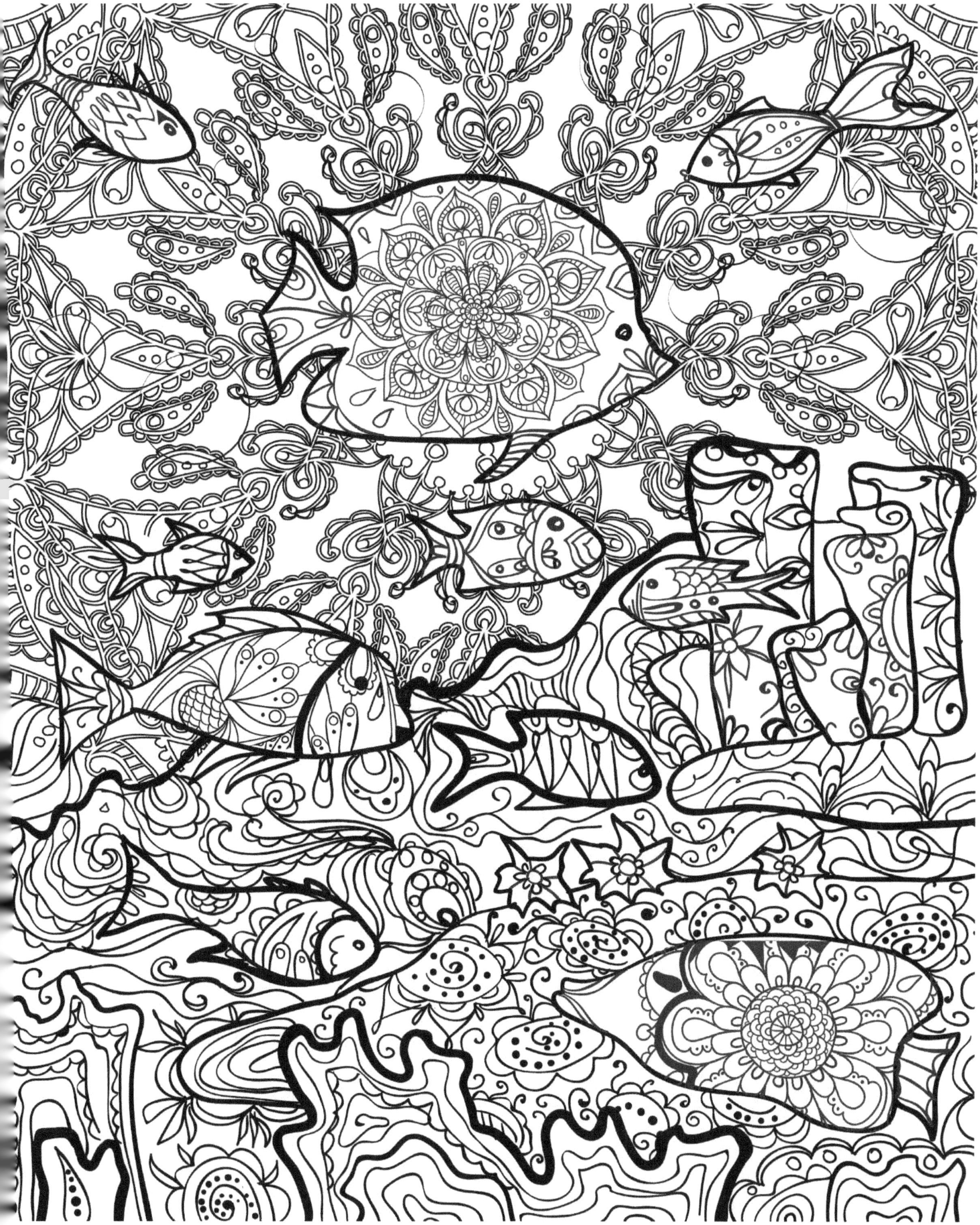

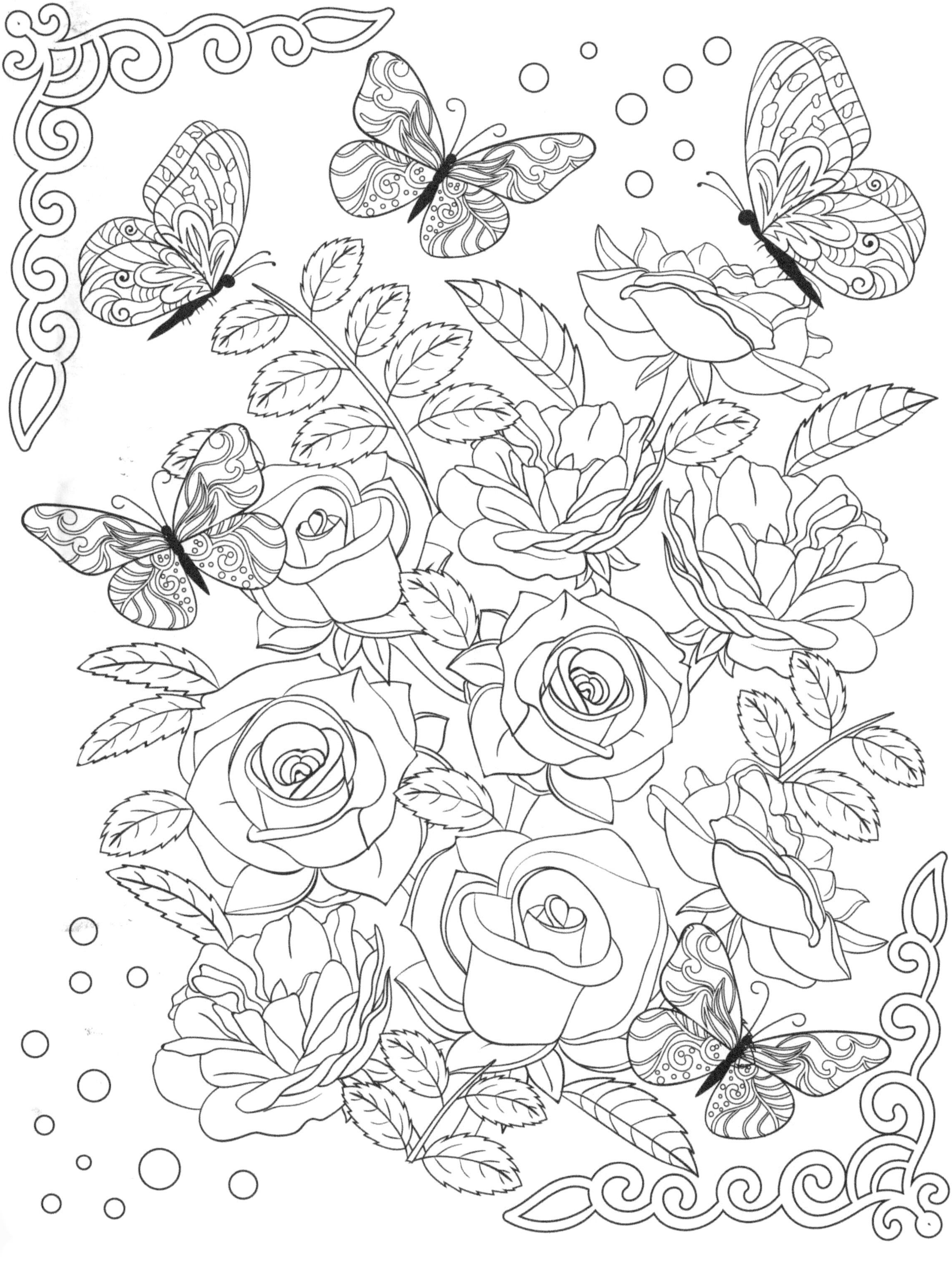

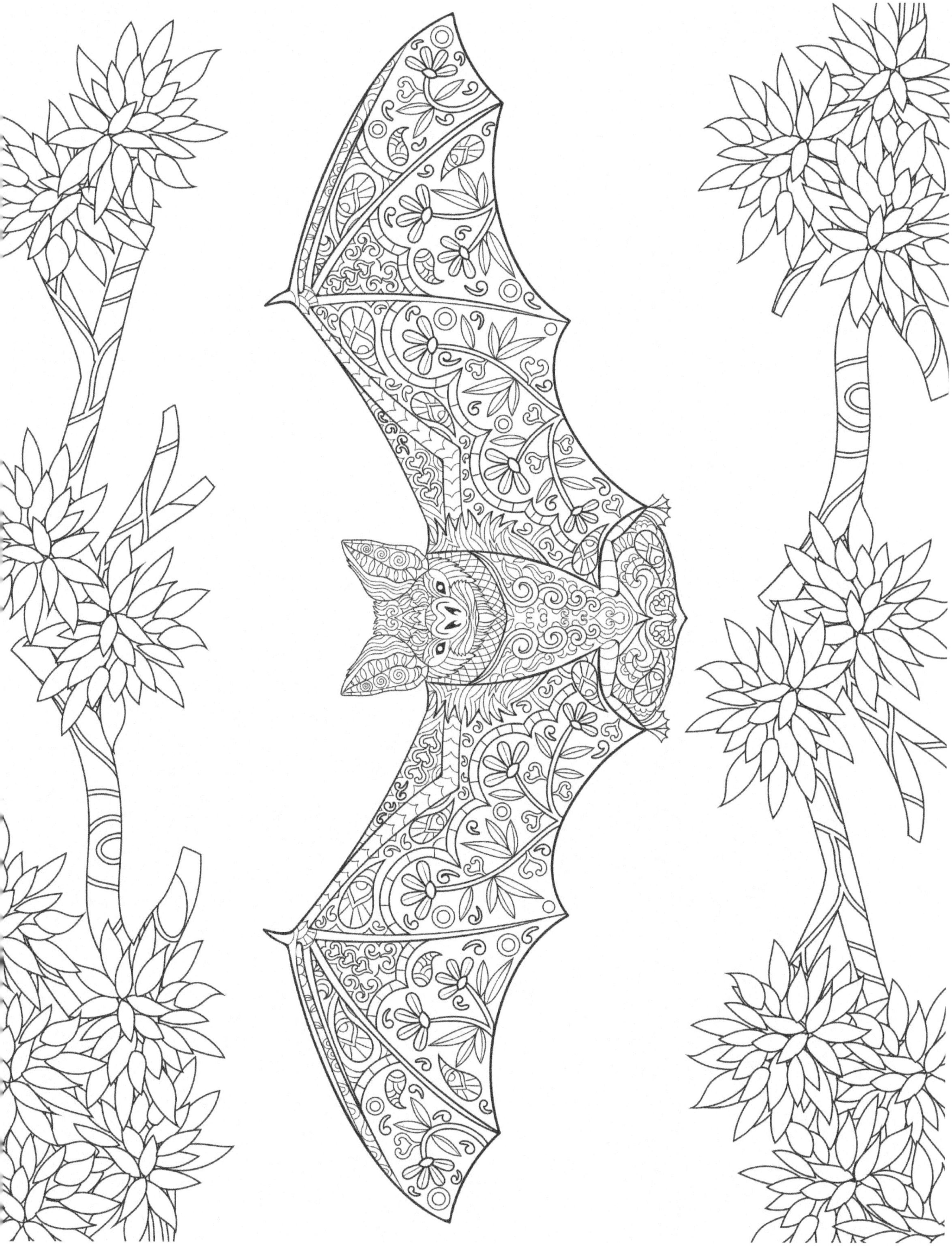

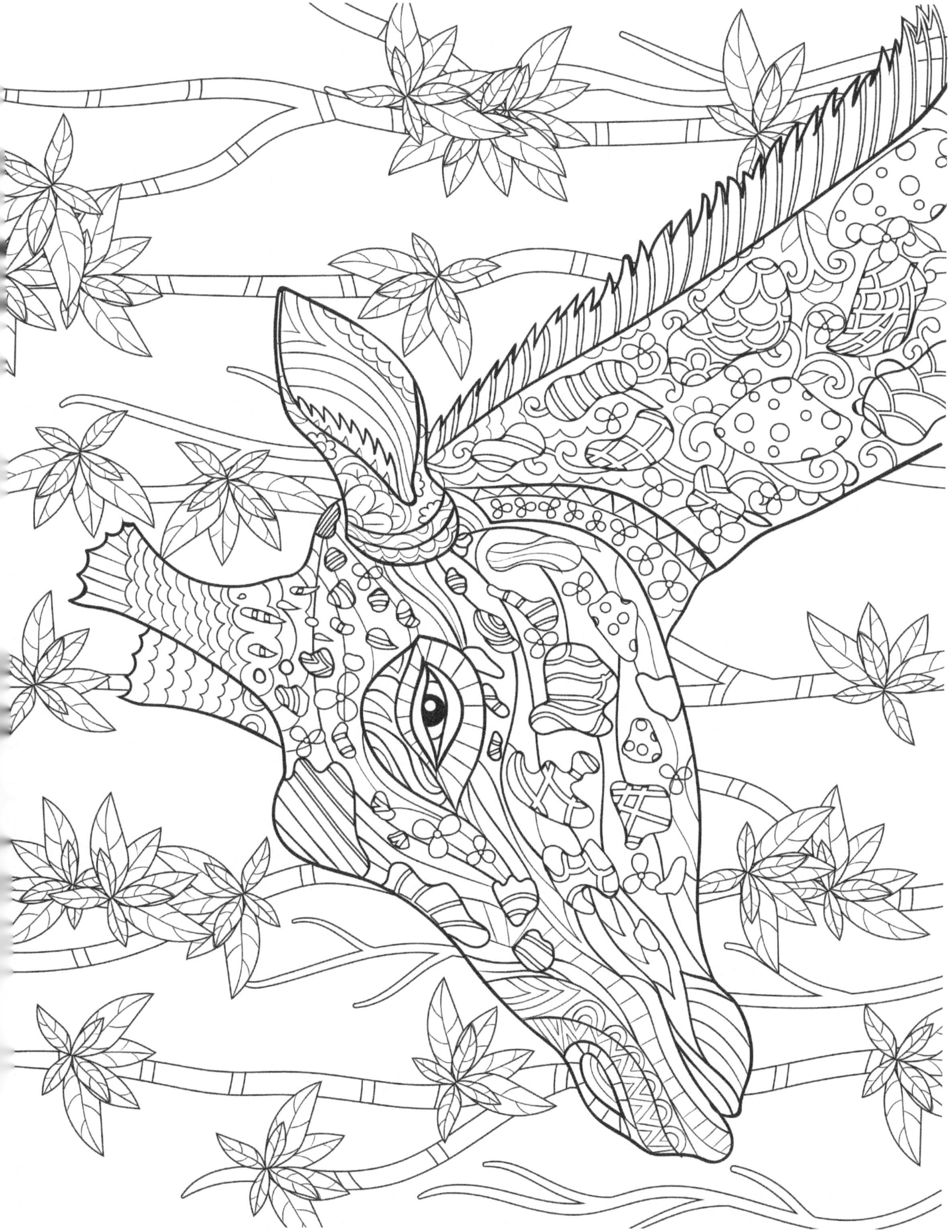

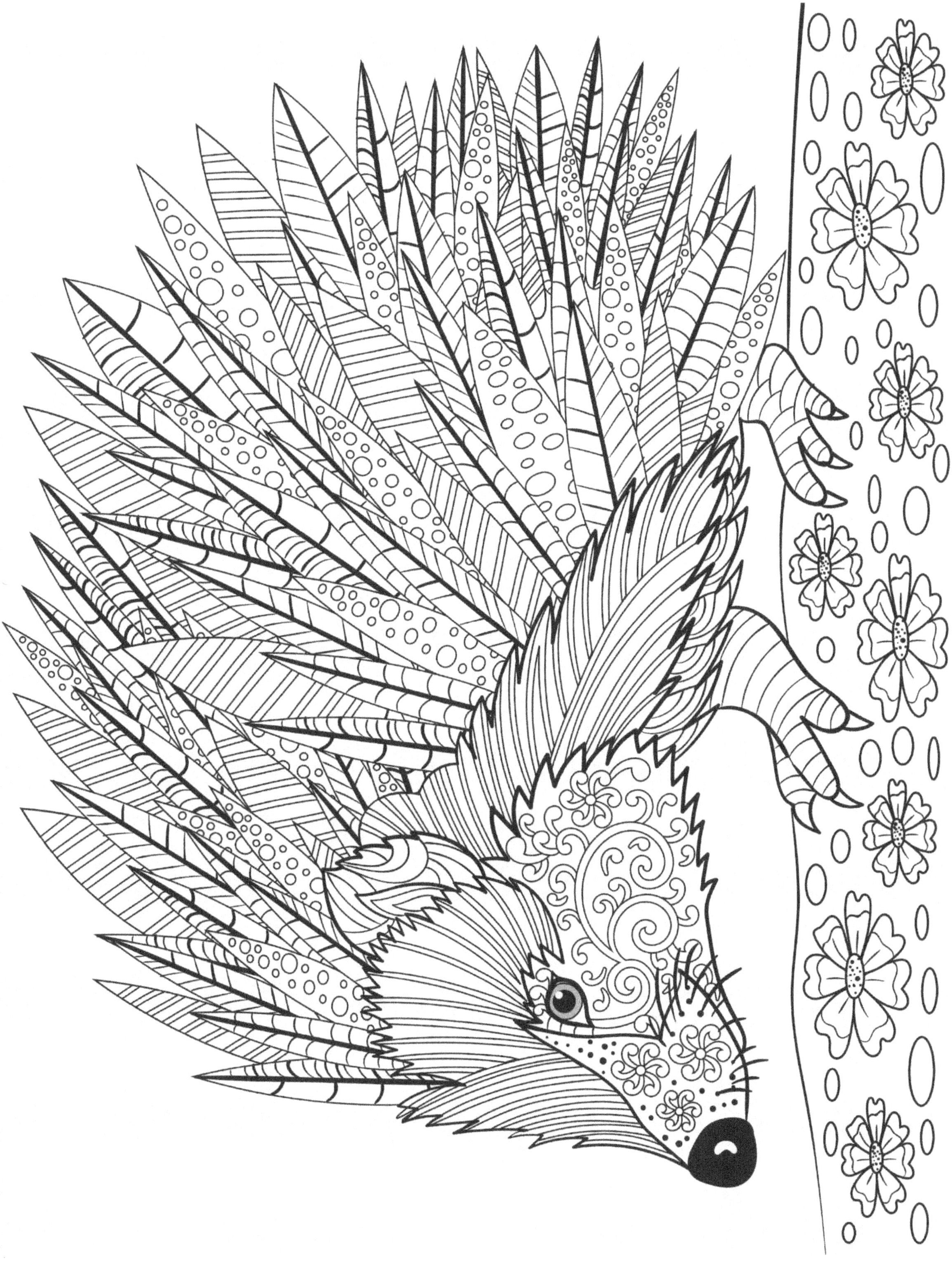

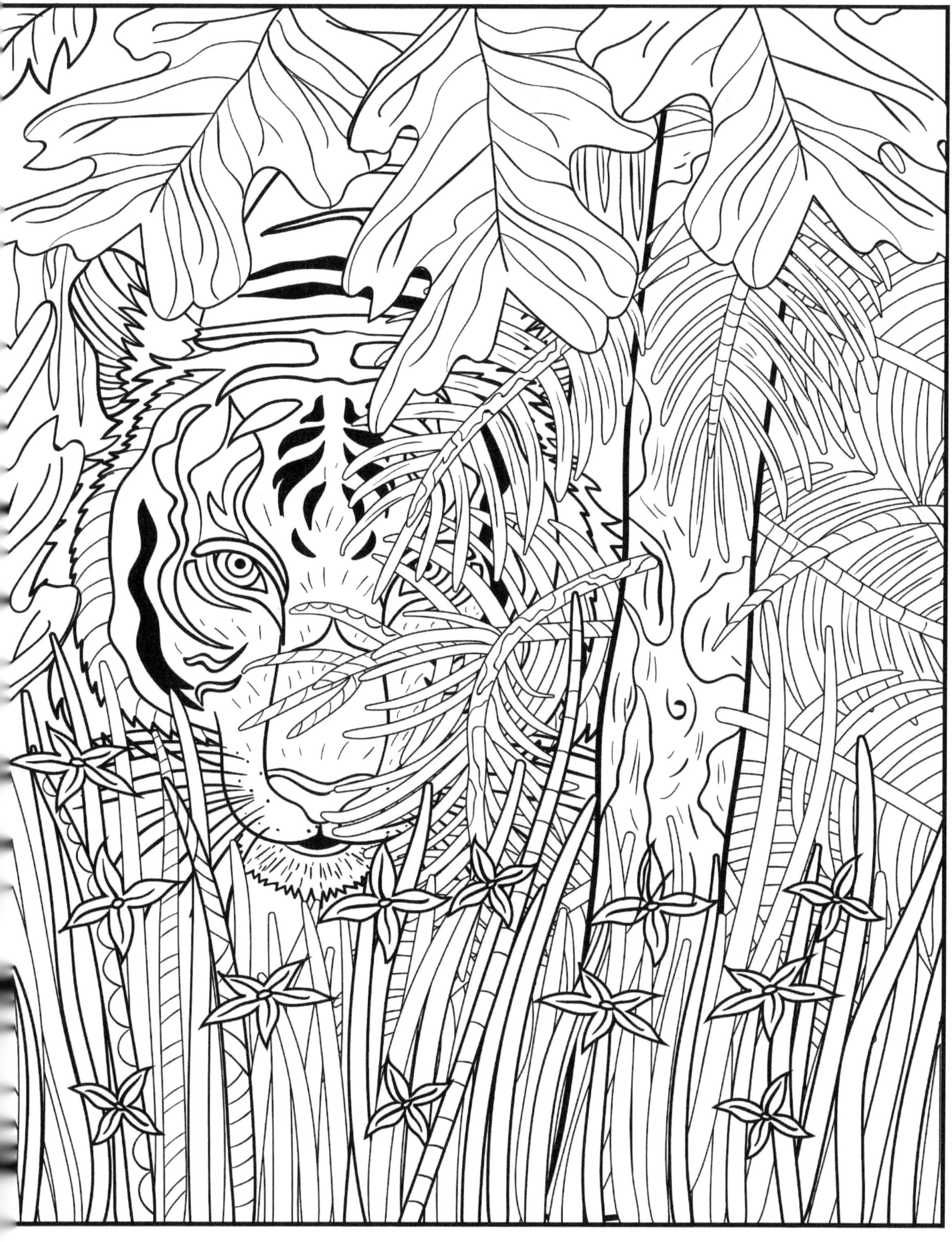

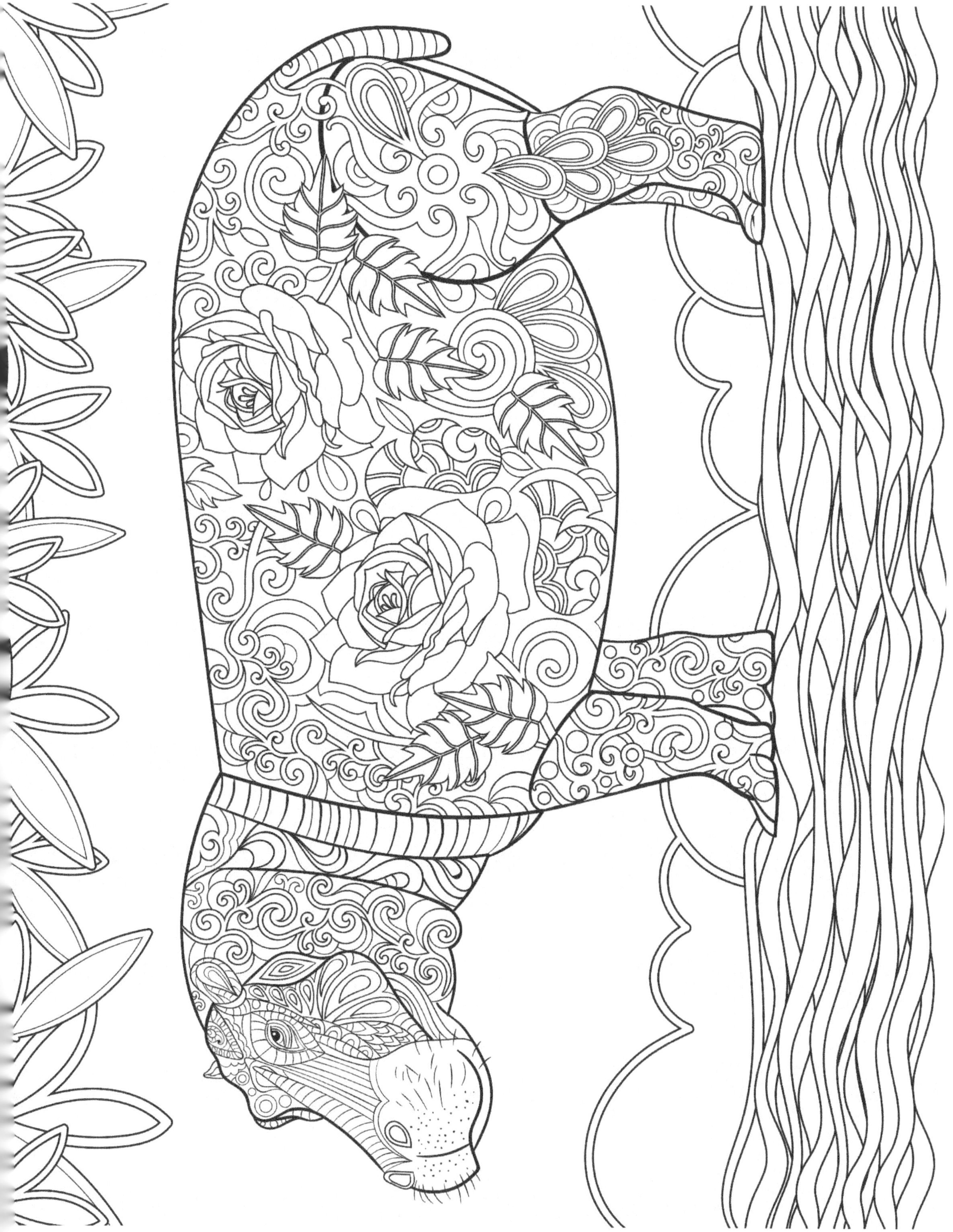

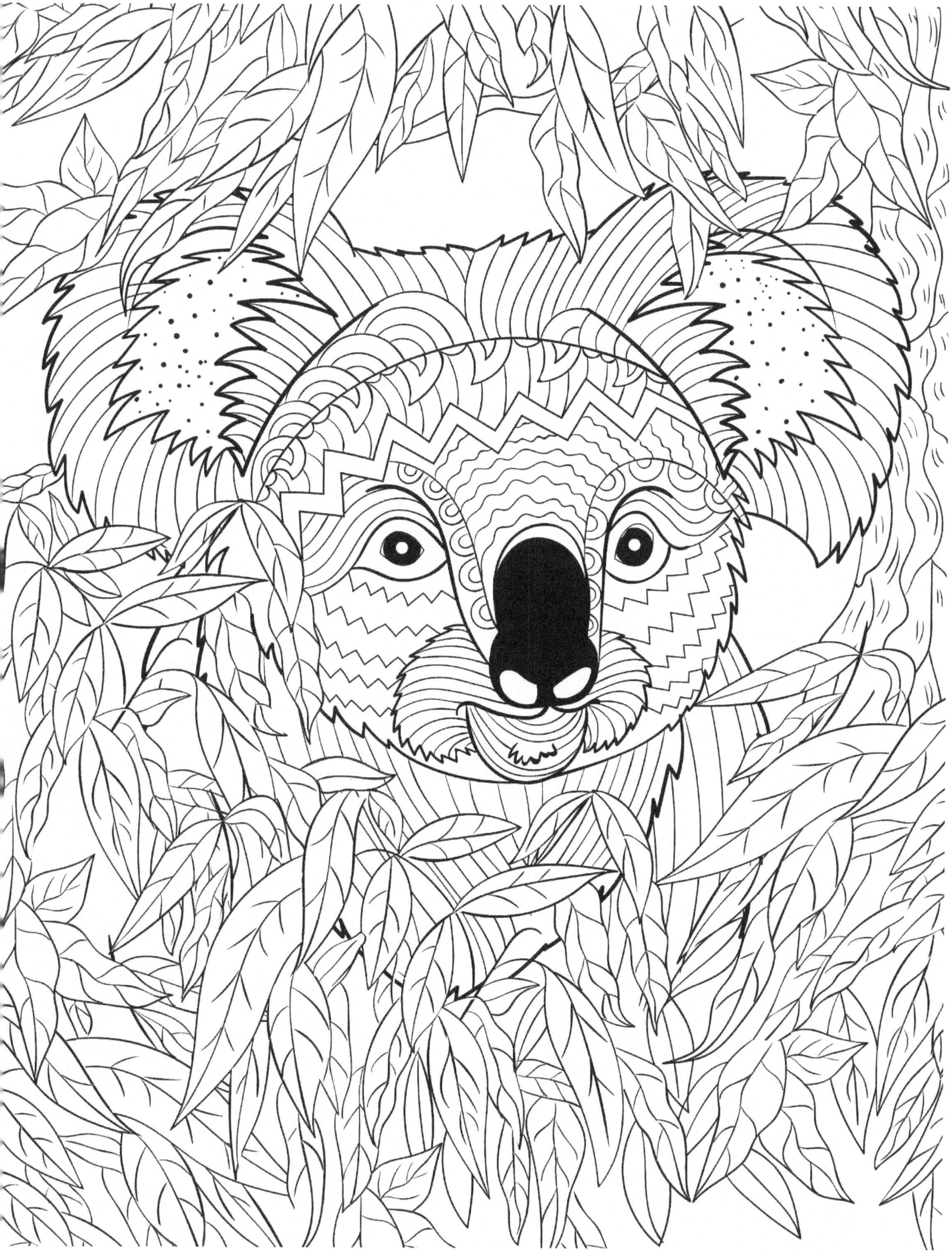

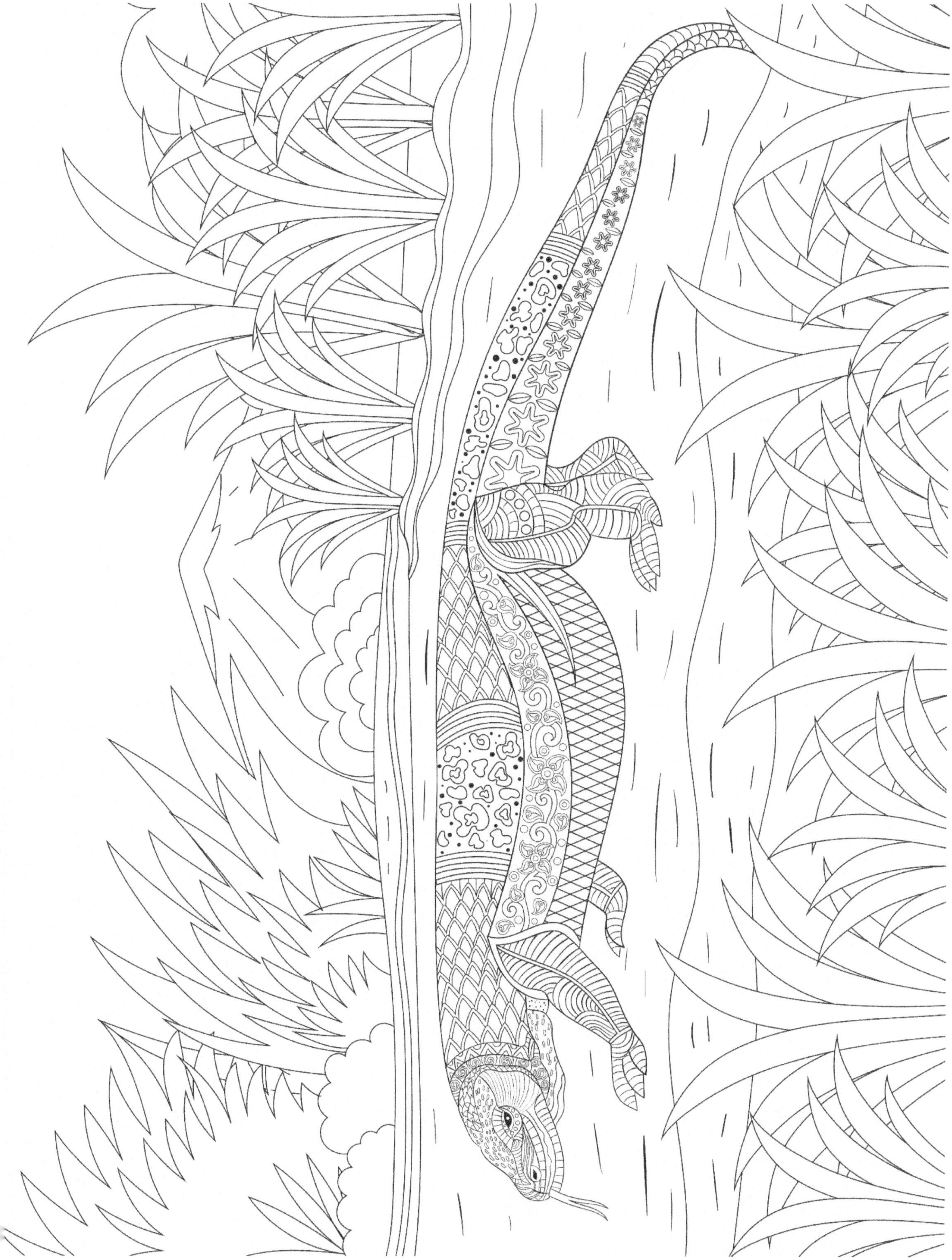

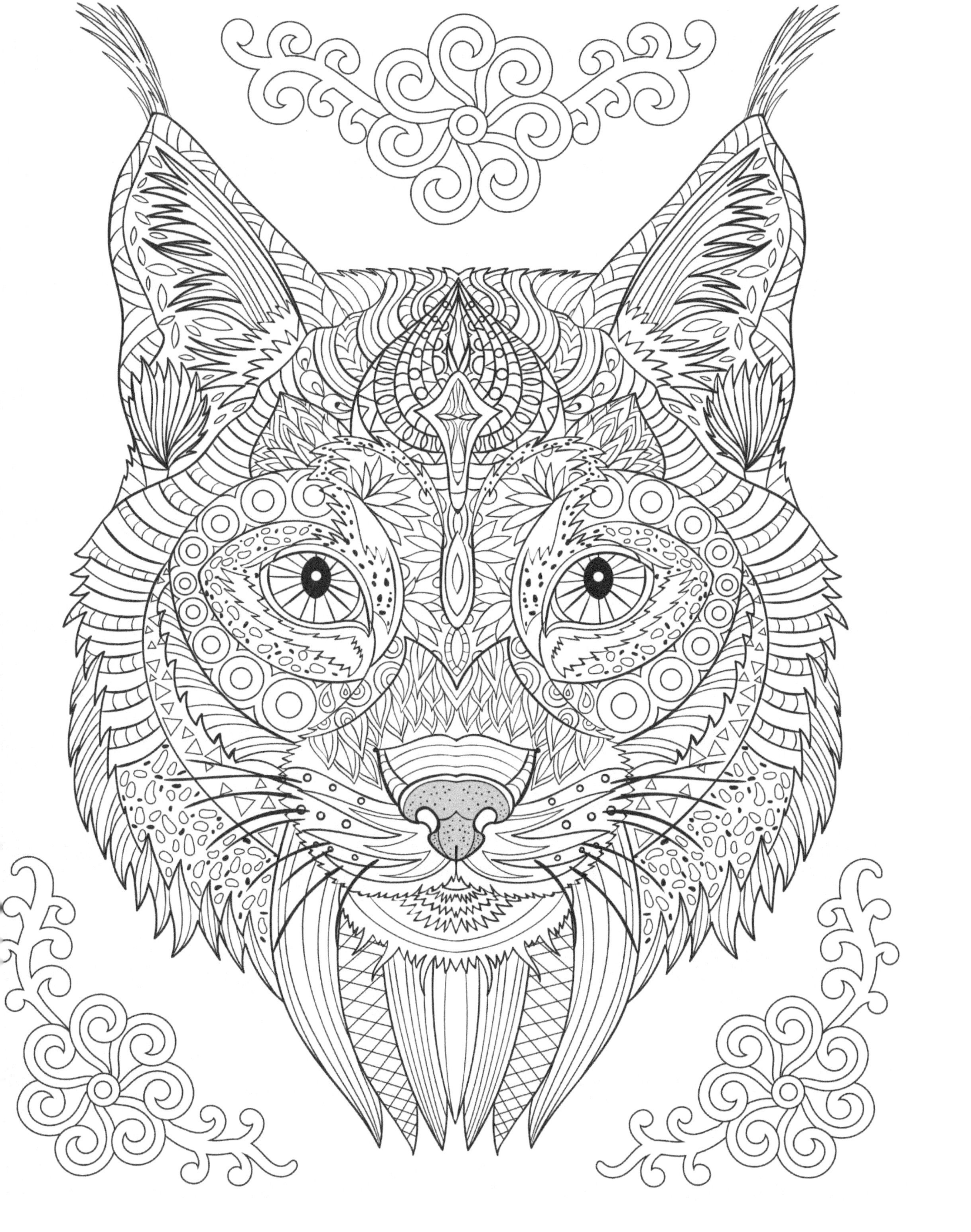

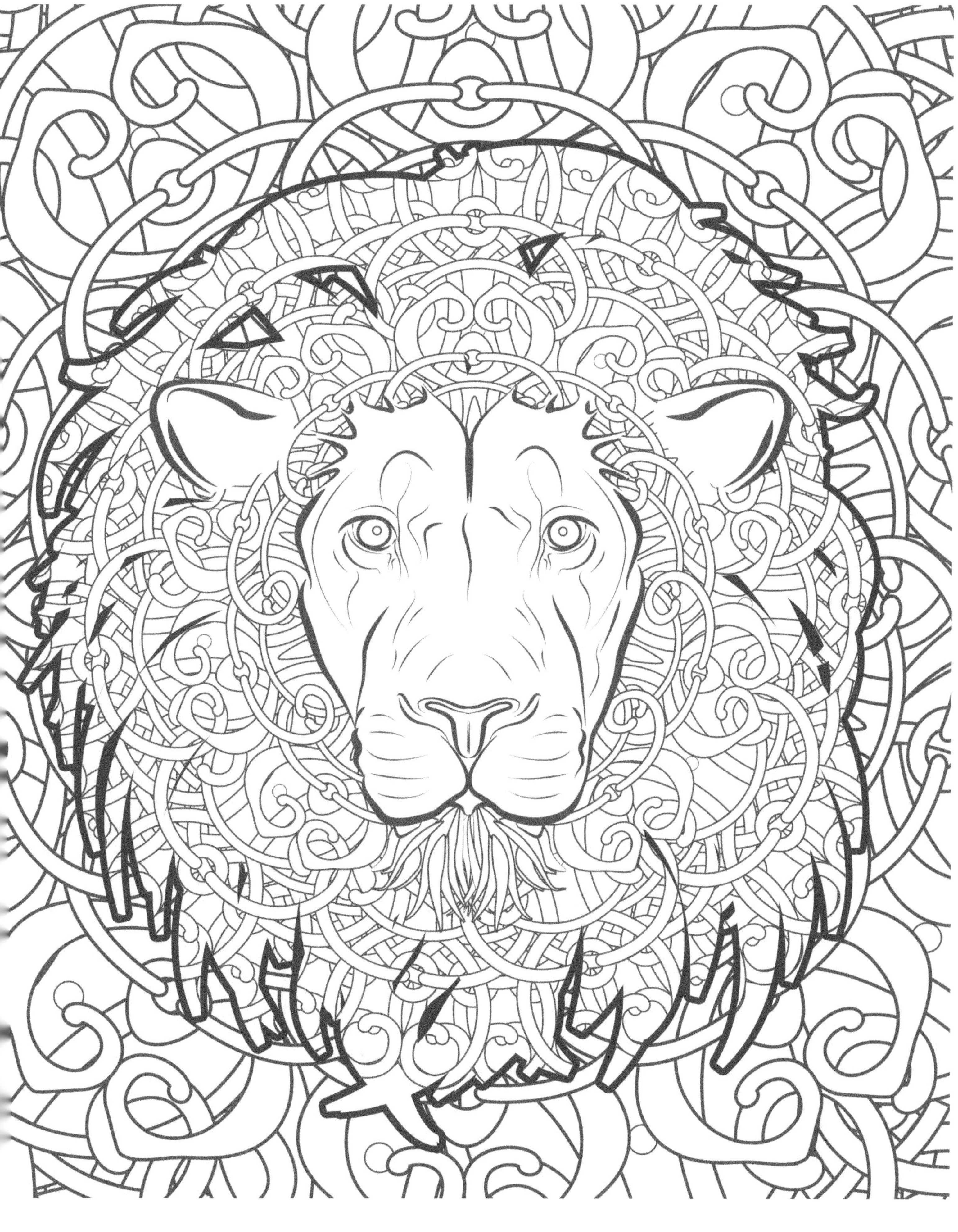

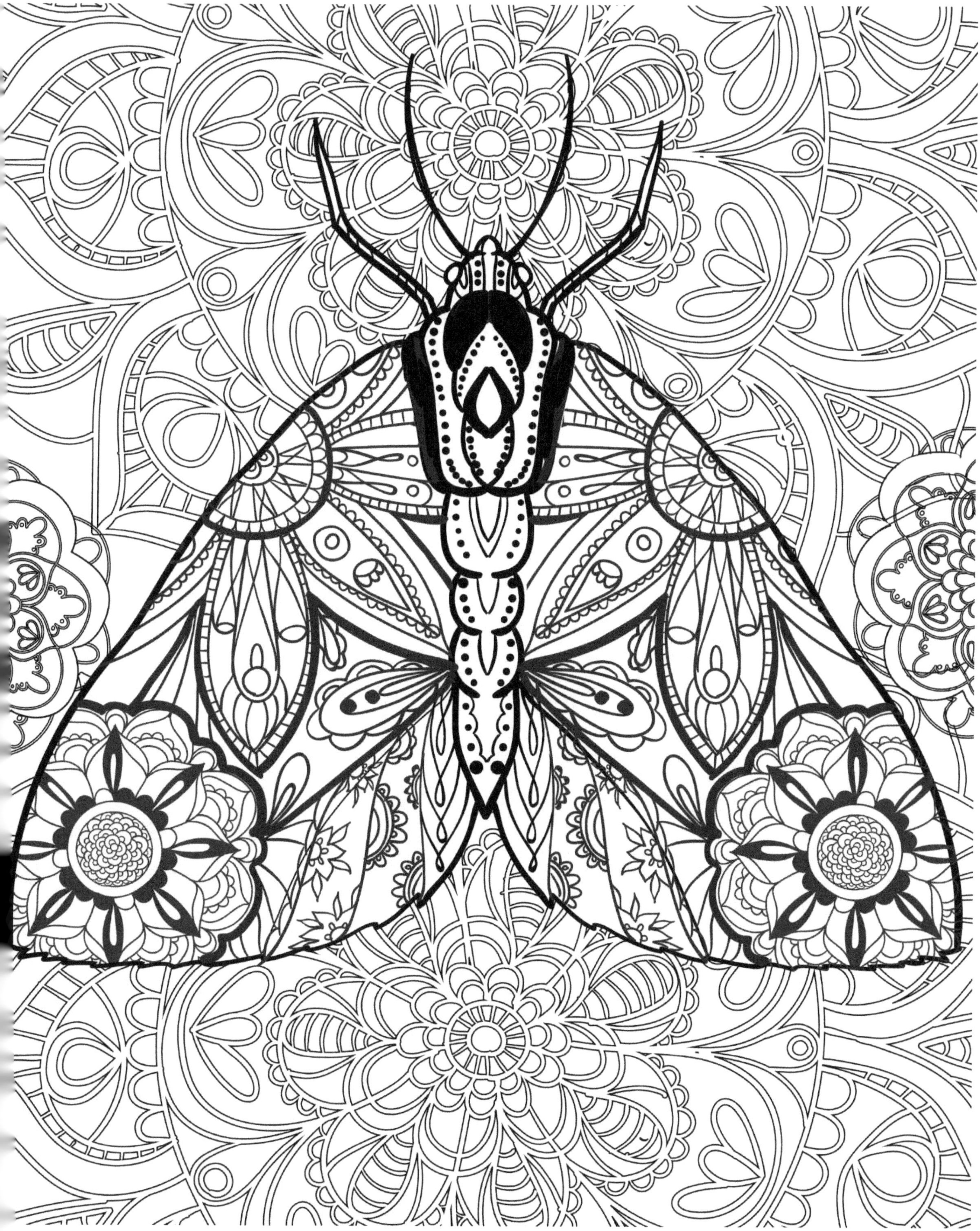

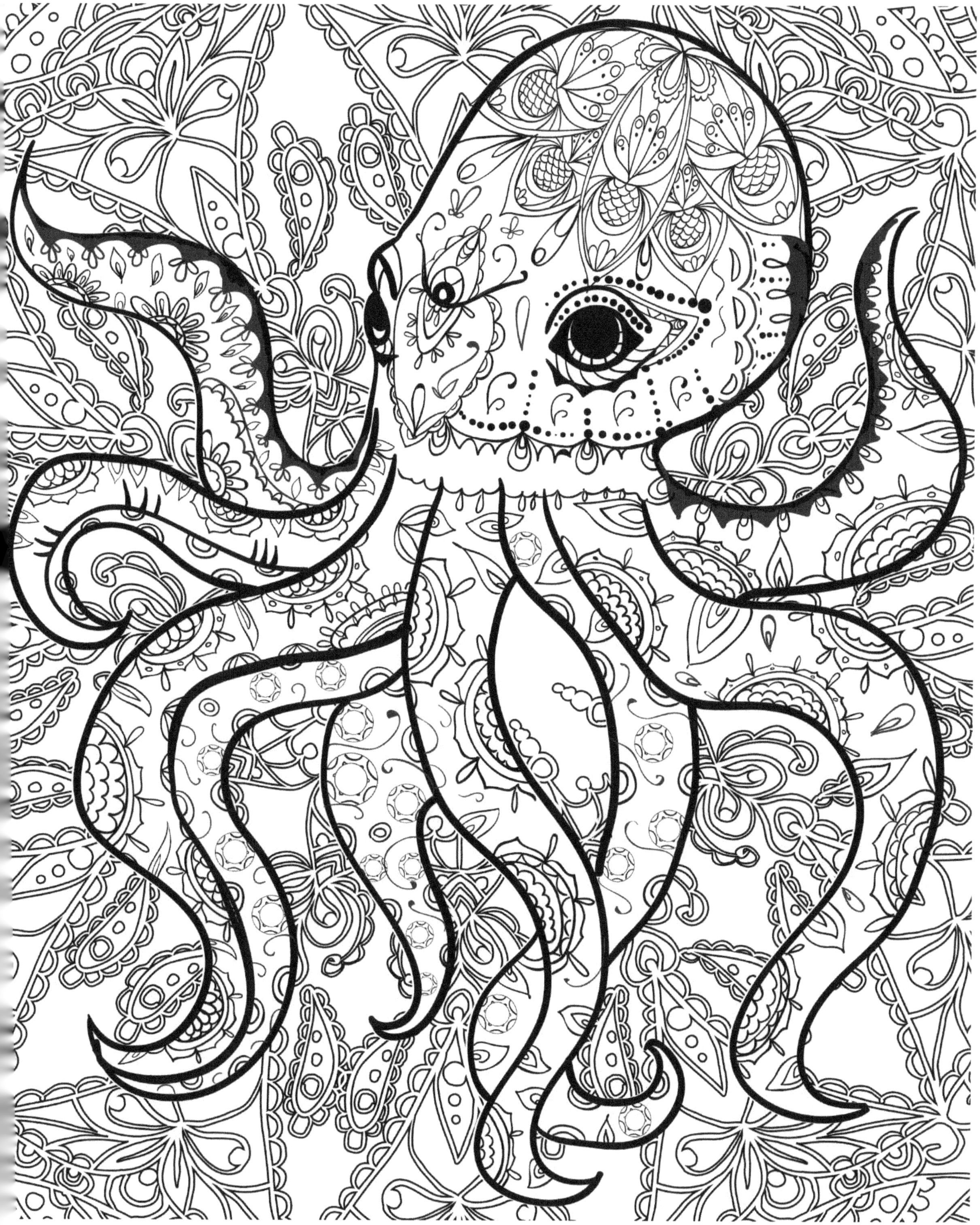

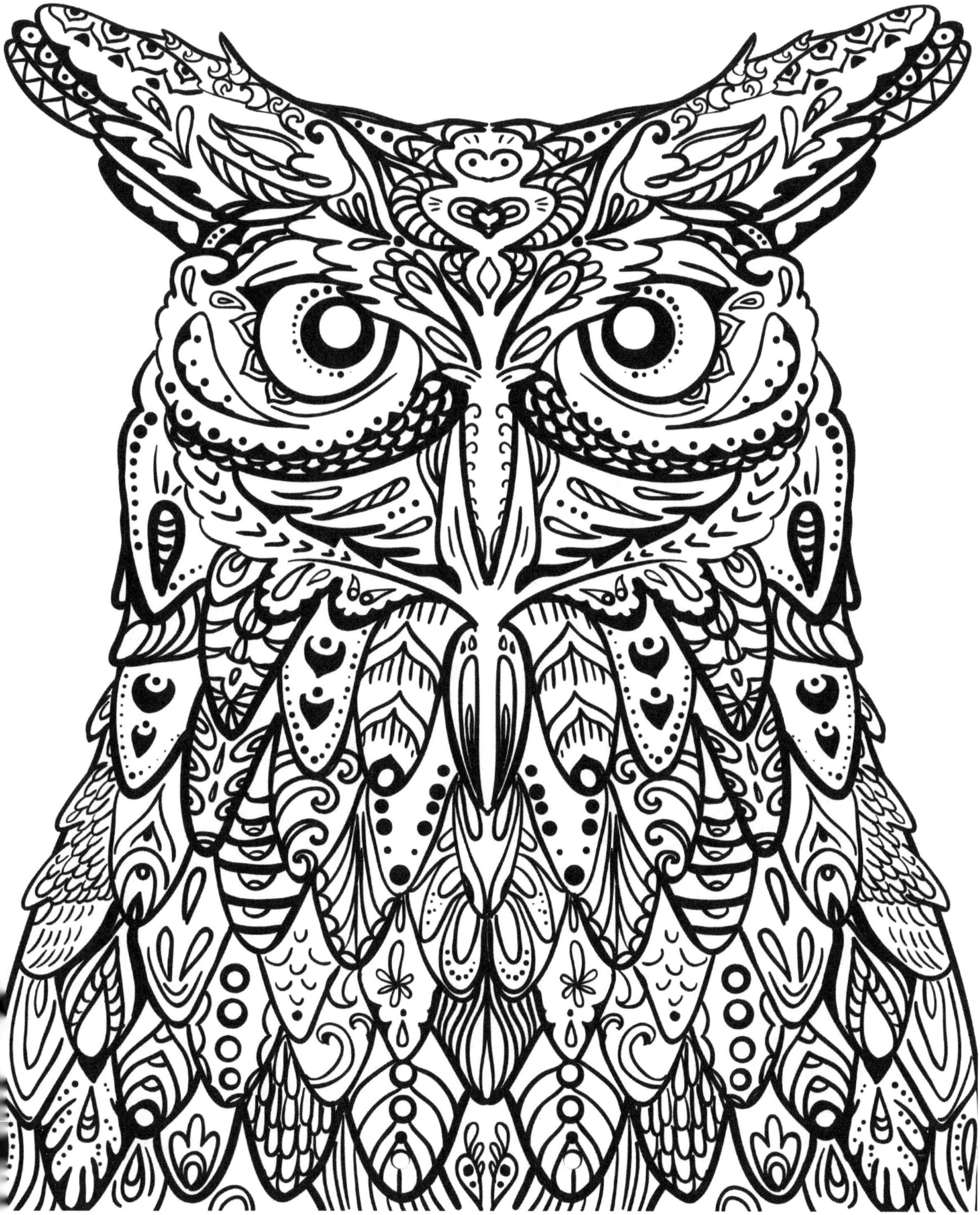

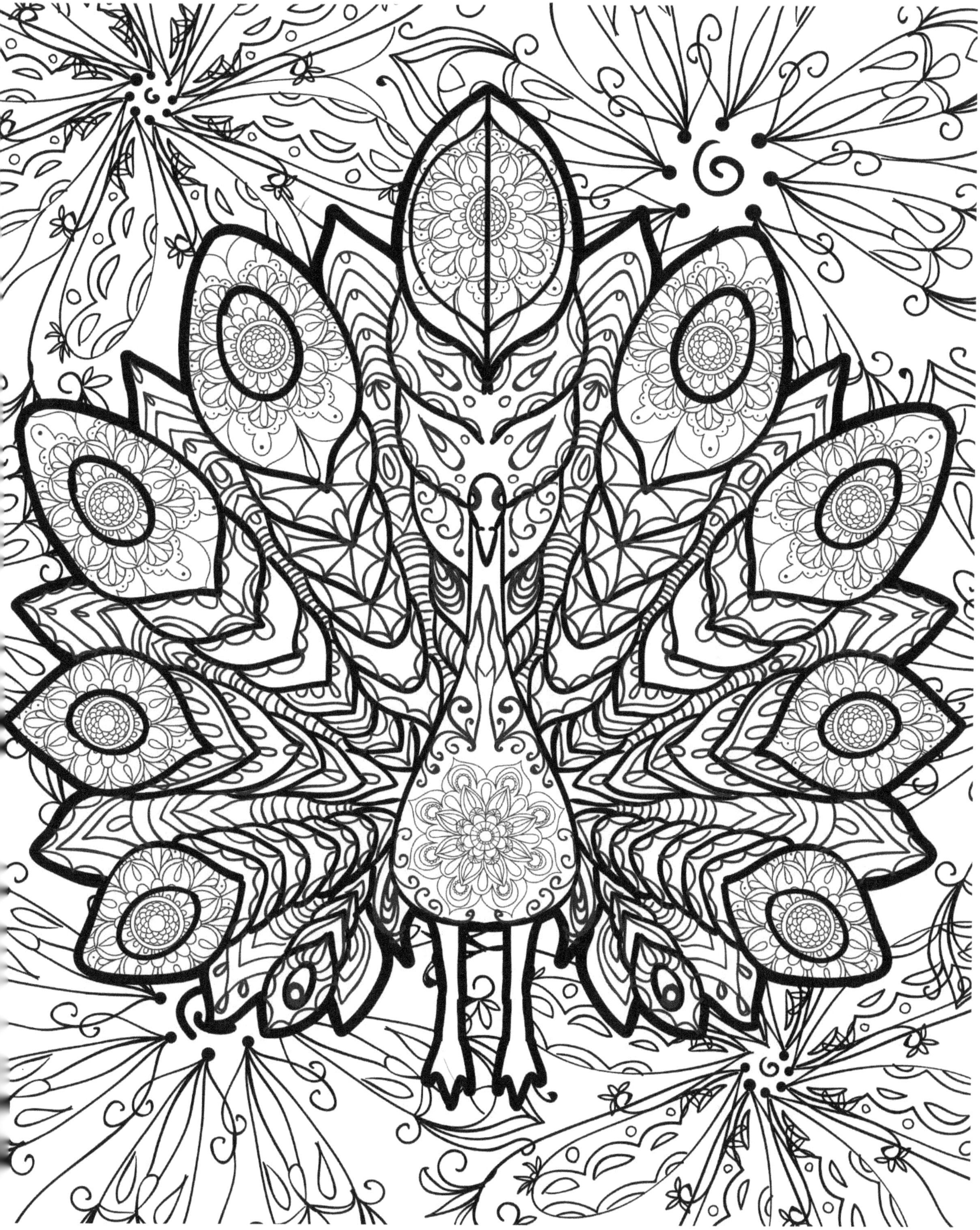

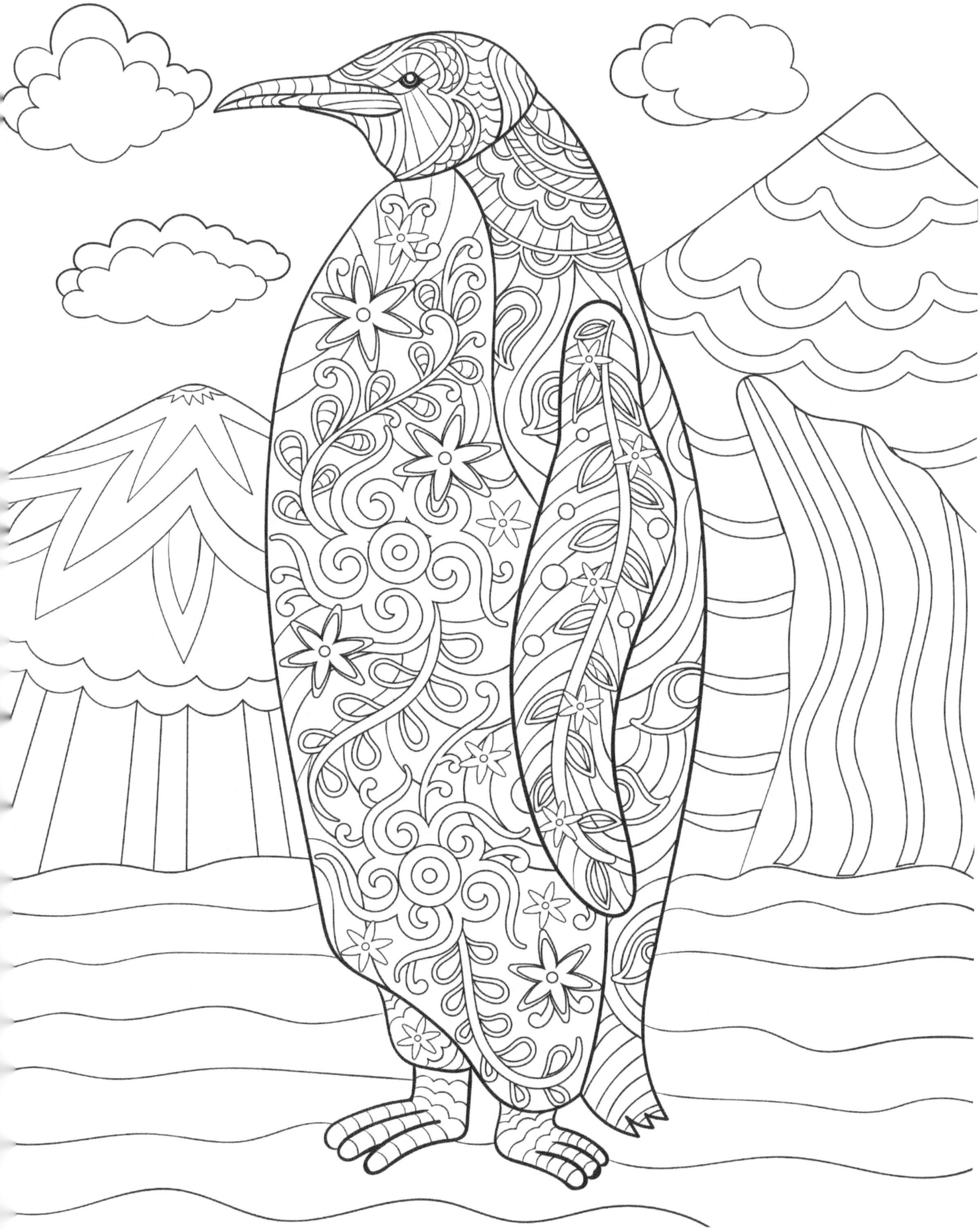

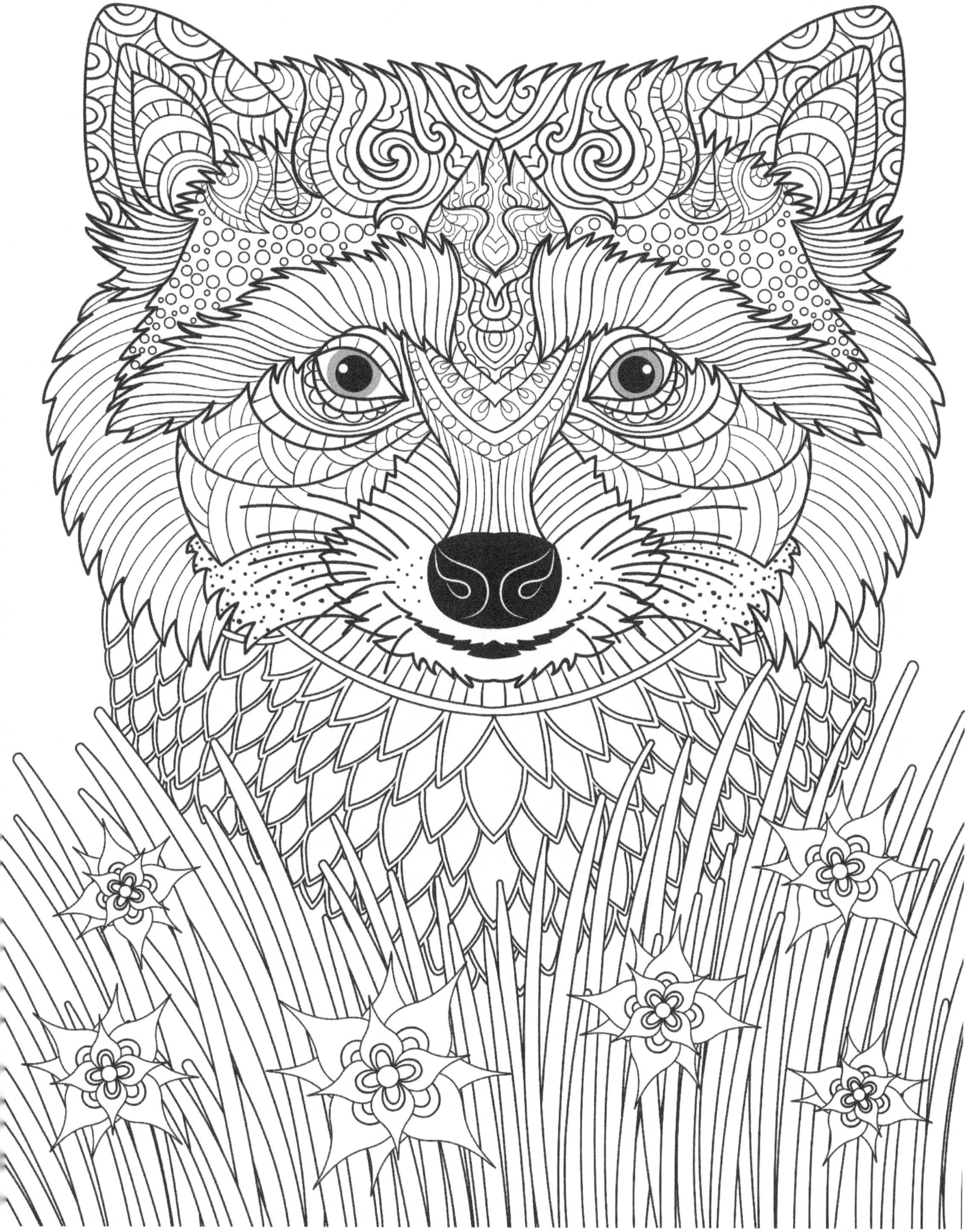

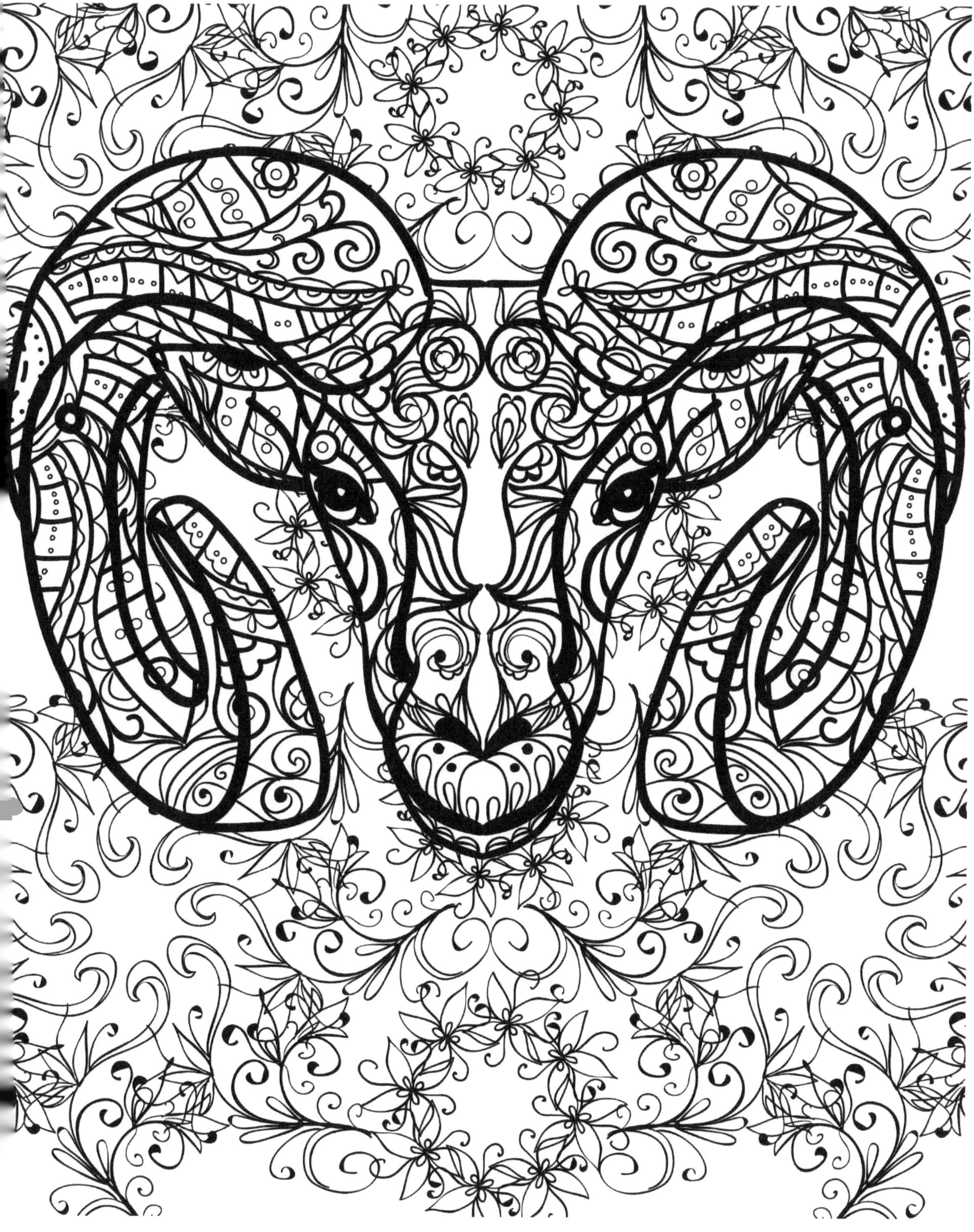

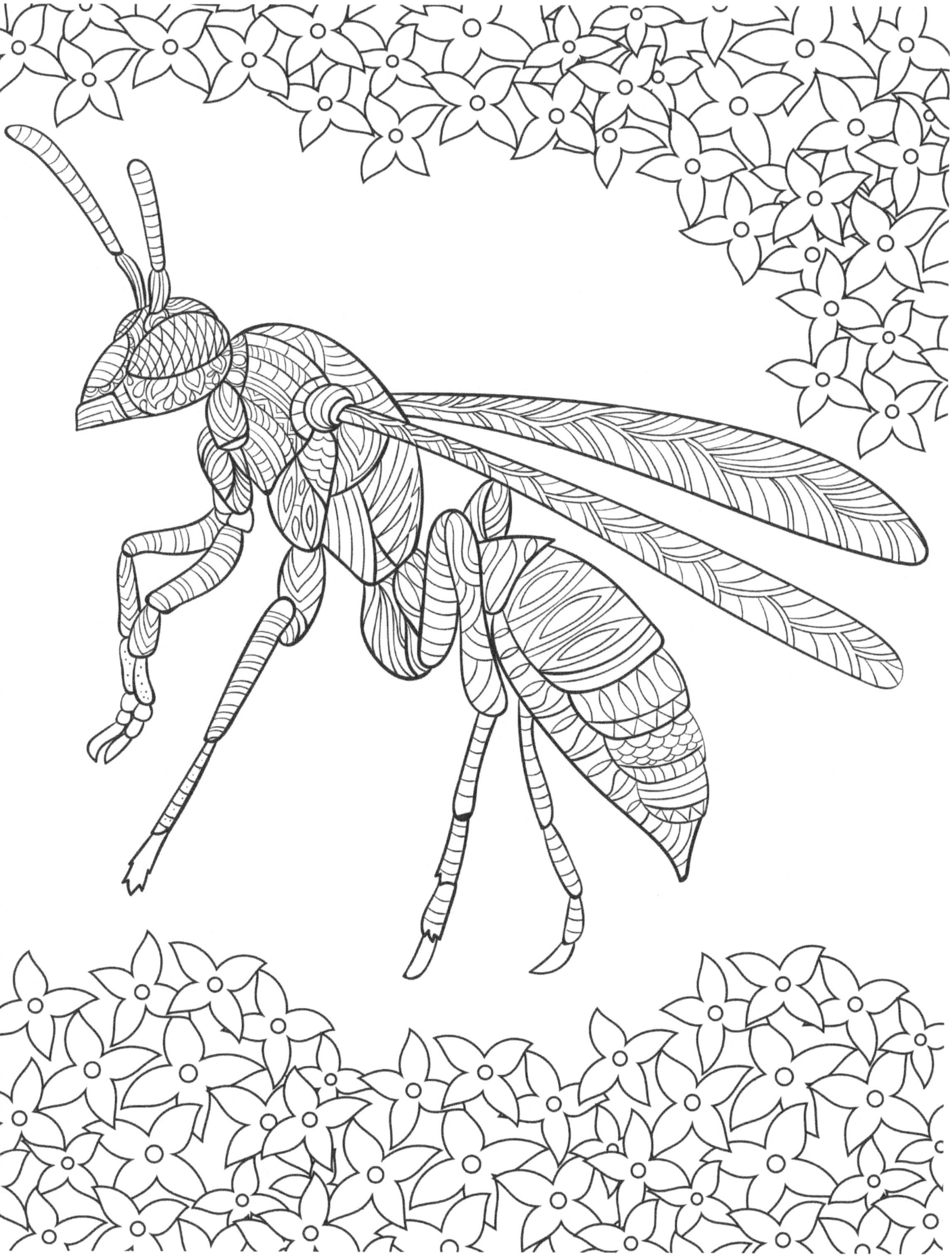

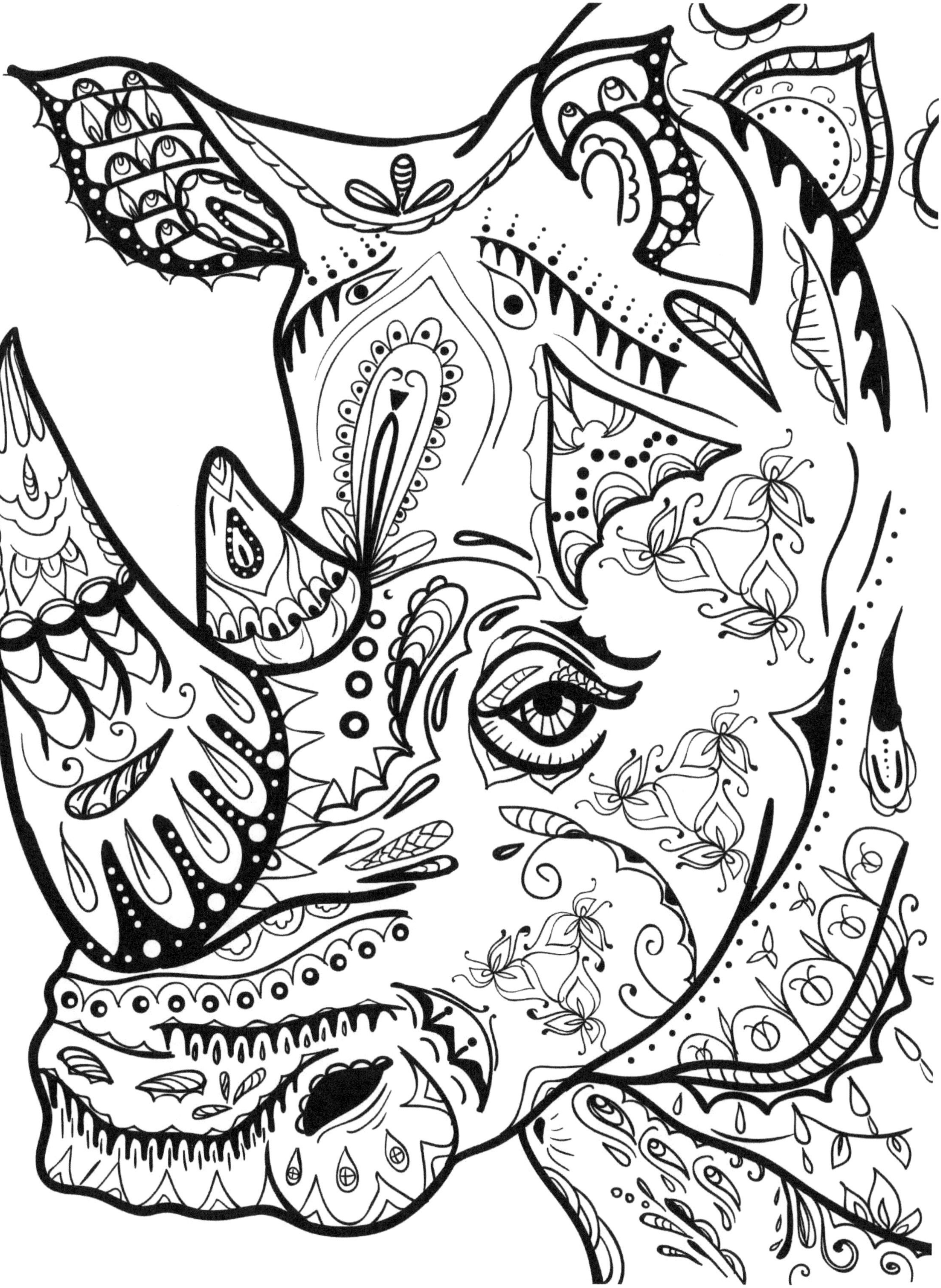

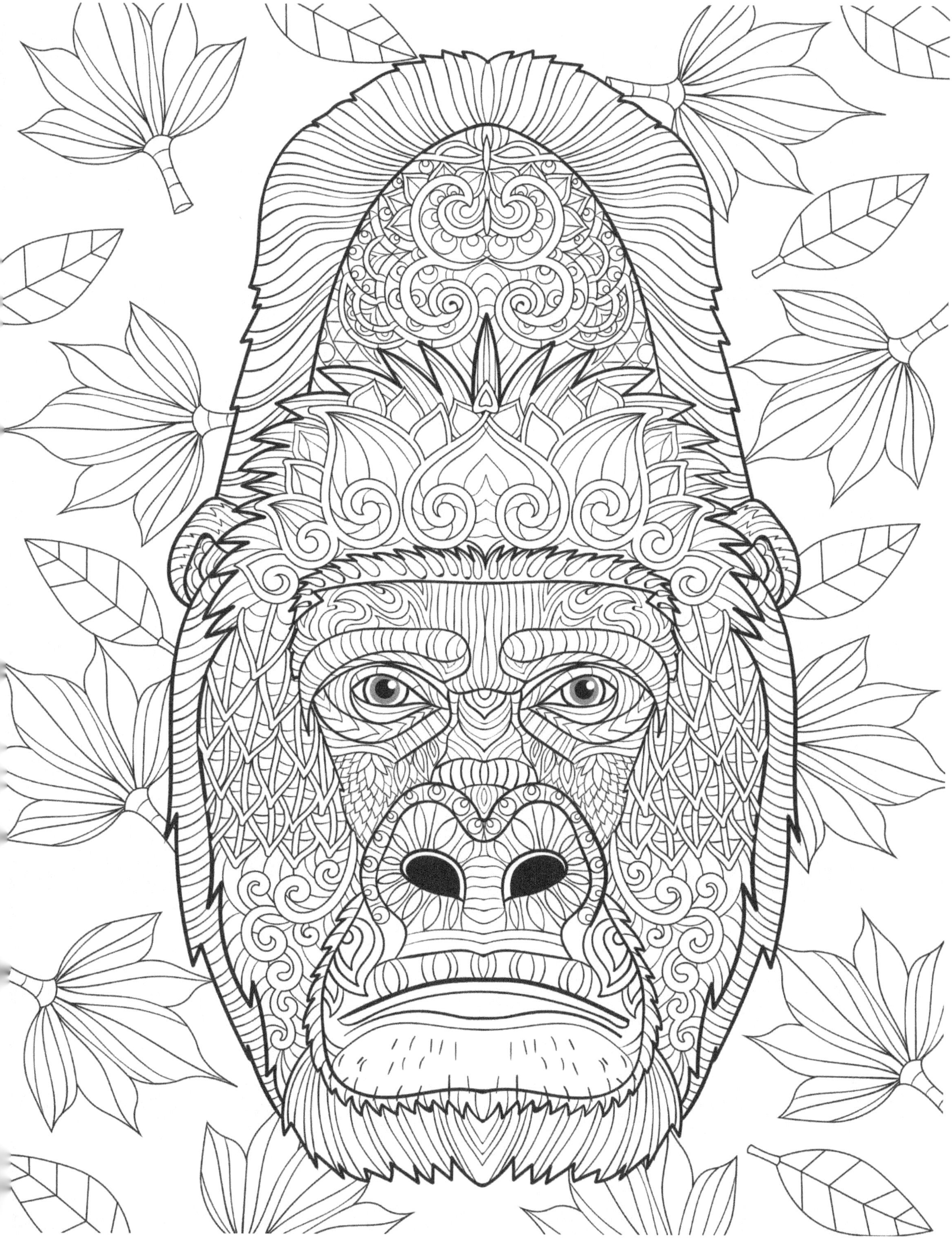

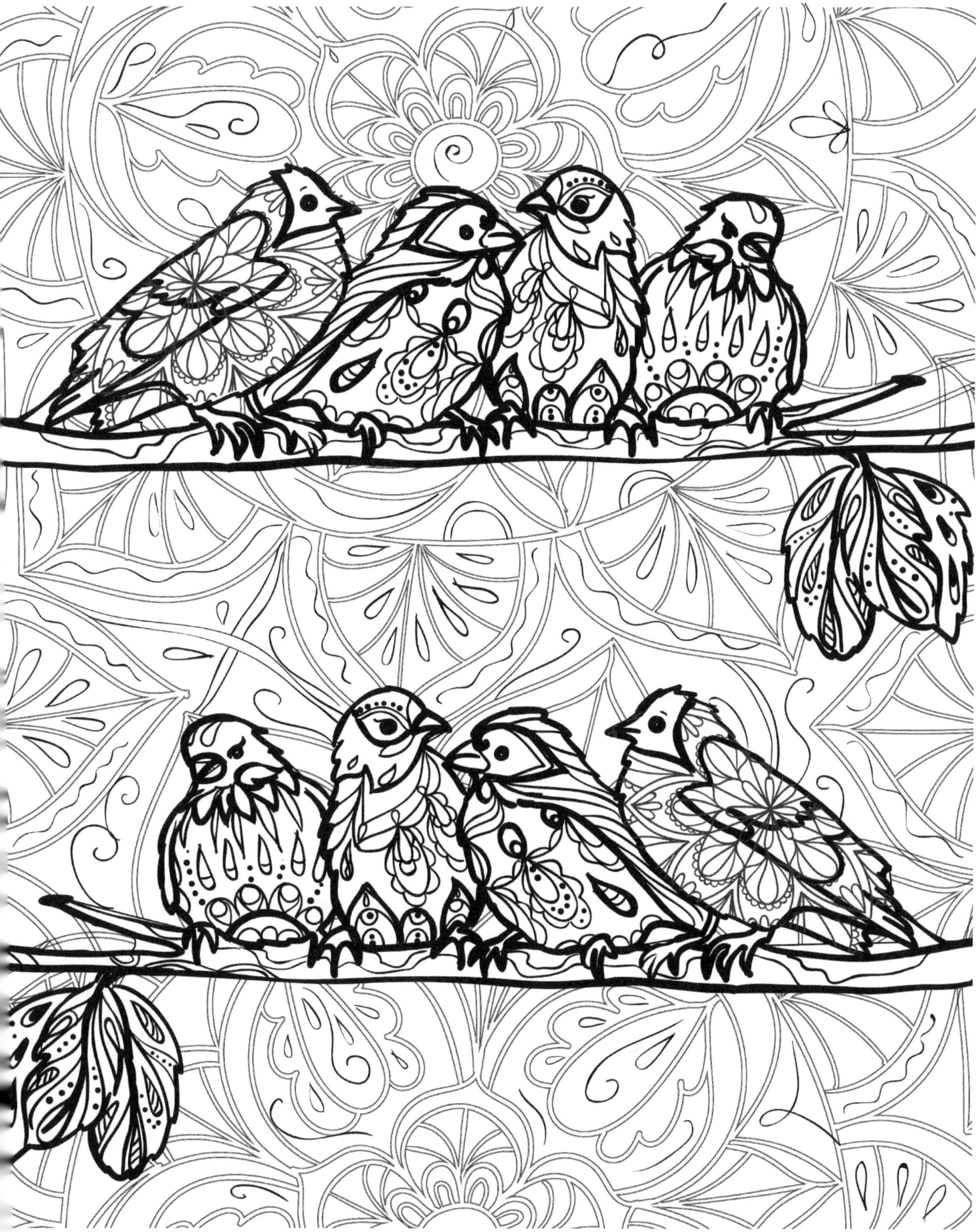

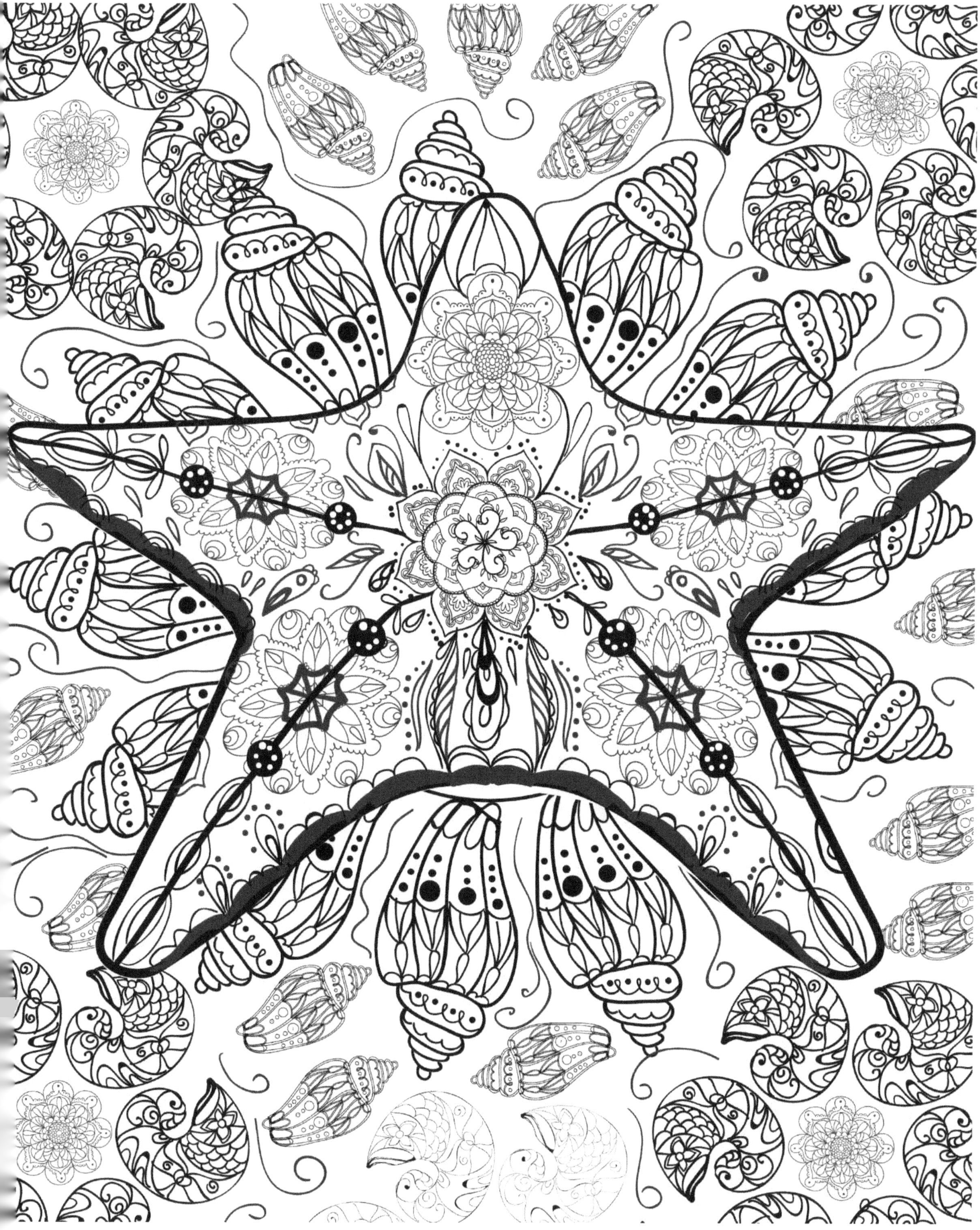

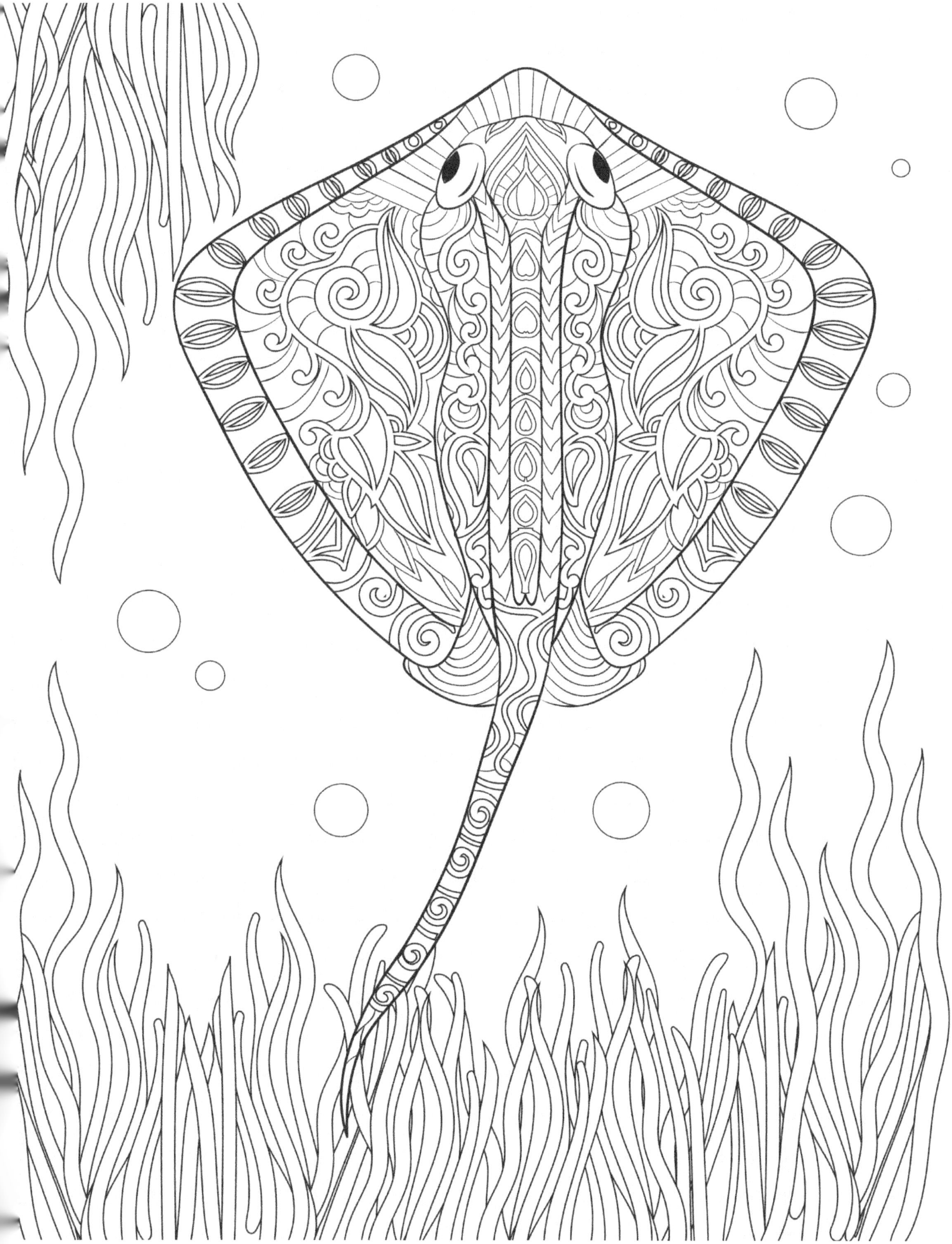

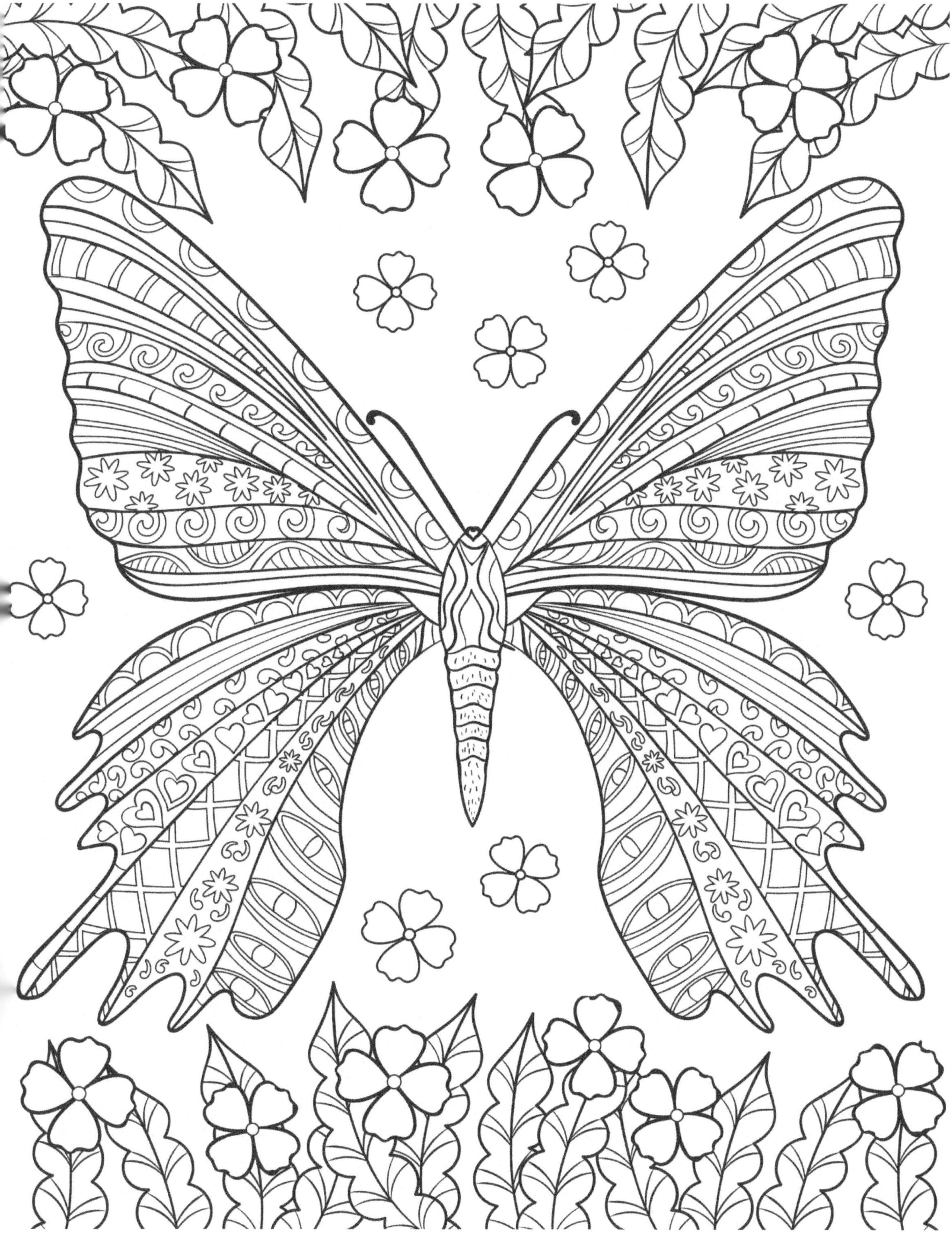

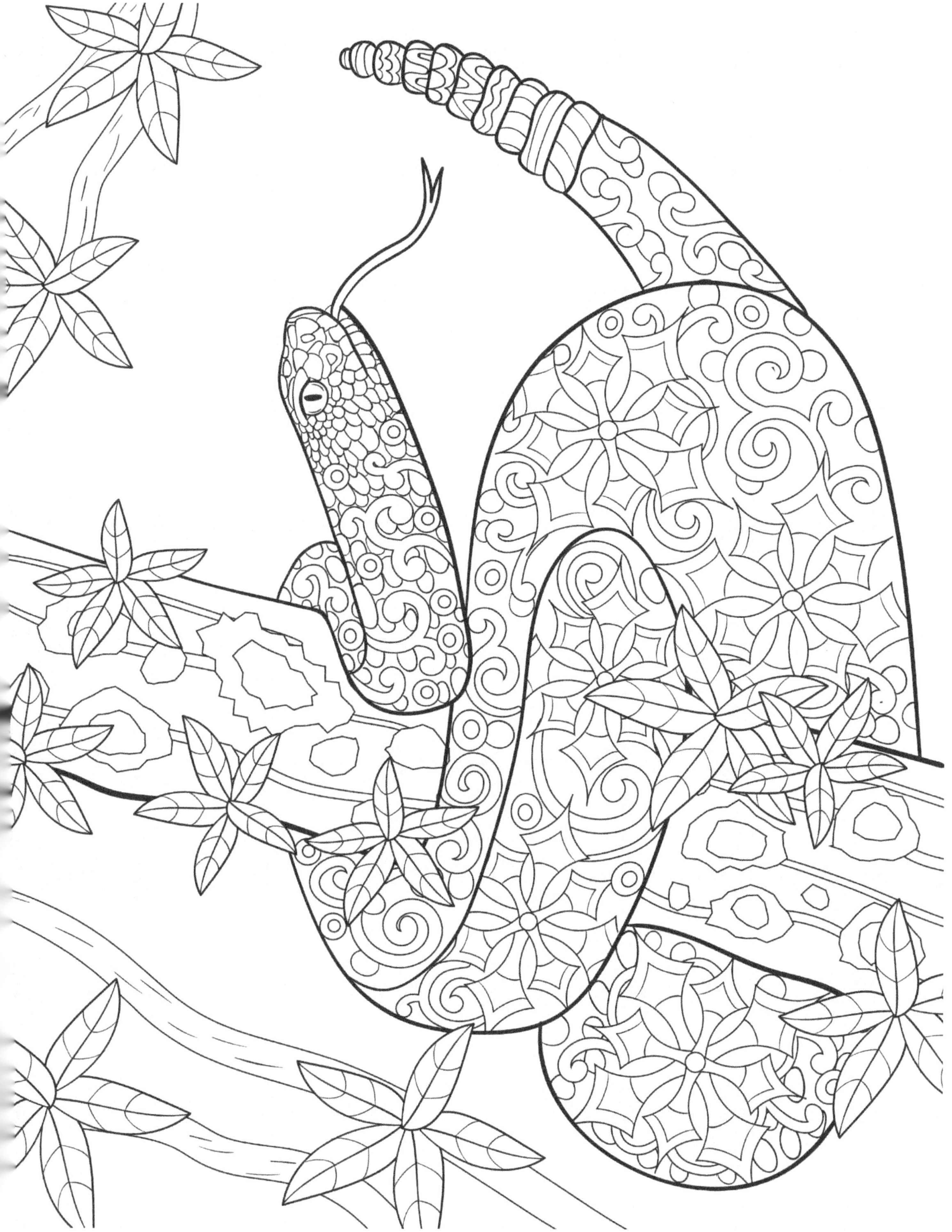

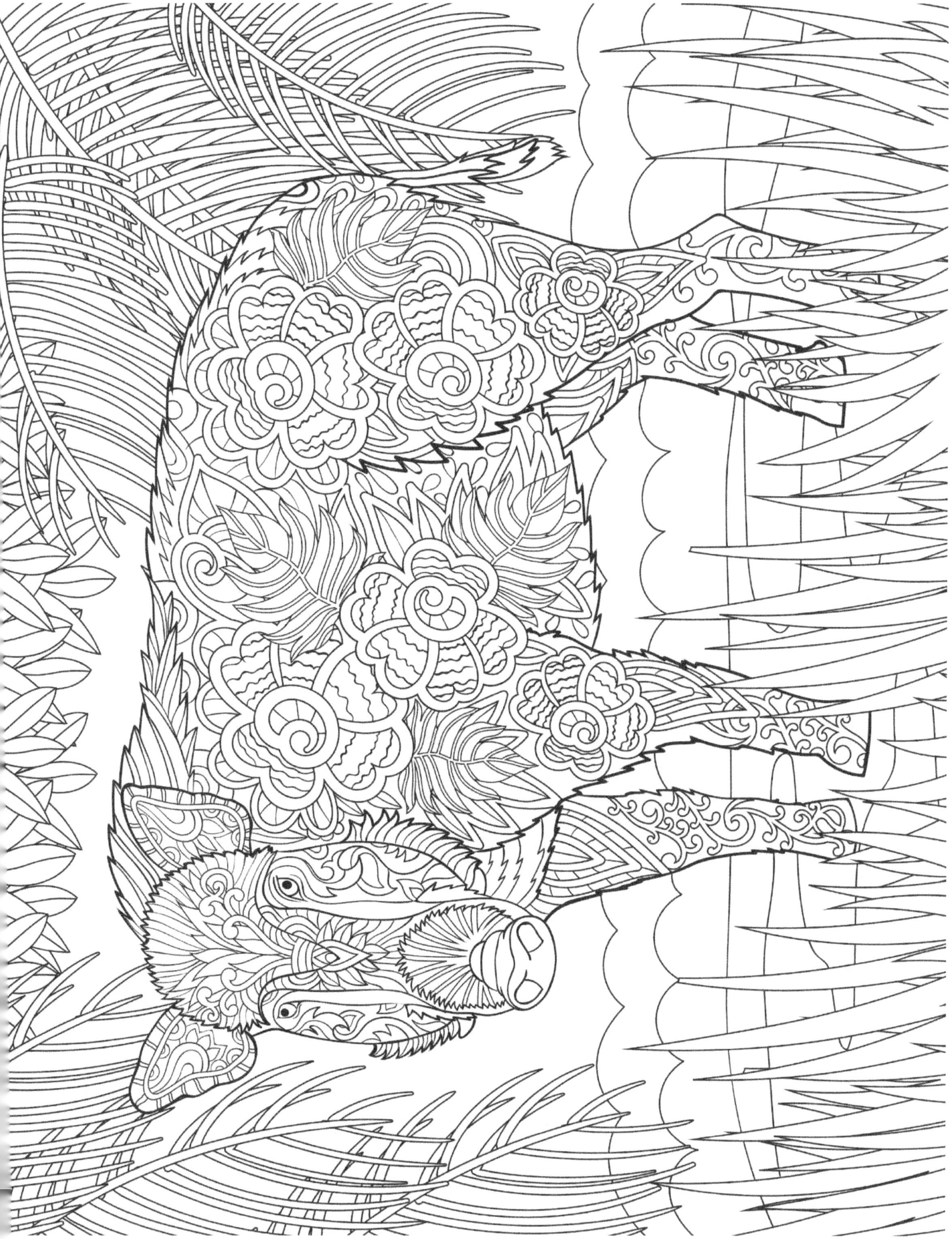

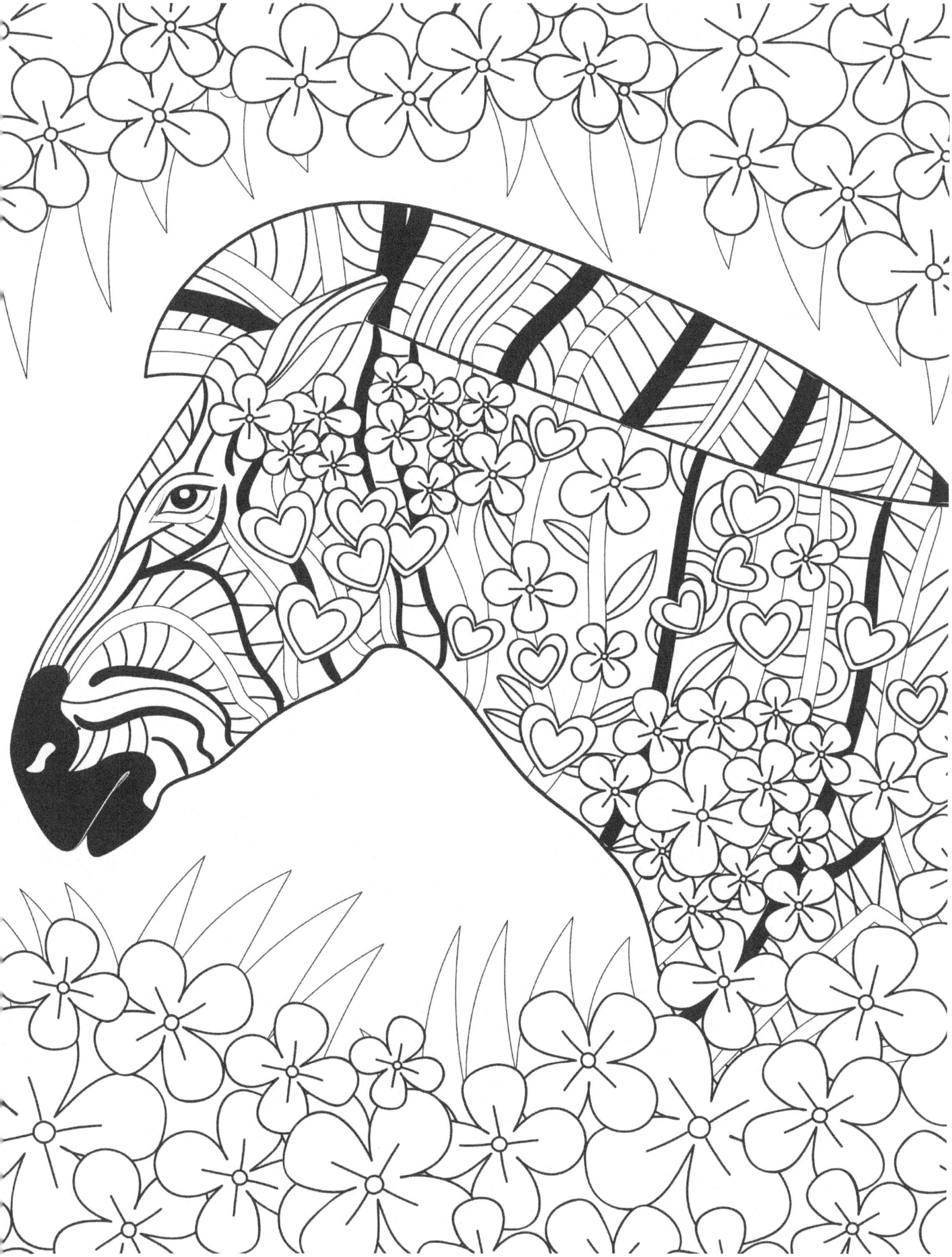

www.ingramcontent.com/pod-product-compliance
Lightning Source LLC
Chambersburg PA
CBHW080709190526
45169CB00006B/2310
9781532856471